LUCAS UNLEASHED

LUCAS UNLEASHED

Wisdom for Life on the High Wire

Jeff Lucas

Authentic
MILTON KEYNES ● COLORADO SPRINGS ● HYDERABAD

Copyright © 2009 Jeff Lucas

15 14 13 12 11 10 09   7 6 5 4 3 2 1

First published 2009 by Authentic Media
9 Holdom Avenue, Bletchley, Milton Keynes, Bucks,
MK1 1QR, UK
1820 Jet Stream Drive, Colorado Springs, USA
Jeedimetla Village, Secunderabad 500 055, A.P., India
www.authenticmedia.co.uk

Authentic Media is a division of IBS-STL U.K., limited by guarantee, with its
Registered Office at Kingstown Broadway, Carlisle, Cumbria CA3 0HA.
Registered in England & Wales No. 1216232. Registered charity 270162

British Library Cataloguing in Publication Data
A catalogue record for this book is available from the British
Library
ISBN-13: 978-1-85078-823-2

Front Cover Polaroid: www.finmacrae.com
Jeff Lucas Portraits: www.richbunce.com

Cover design Moose77
Print Management by Adare
Printed in the UK by J F Print Ltd., Sparkford, Somerset

To David Wilkes (1947–2008) who journeyed with
great grace and courage on a dark pathway.
And to dear Annie, his 'rock'

Contents

❦ CONTENTS ❦

Introduction

The conversation had a furtive feel about it, as if we were talking about something frightfully naughty. This behind-cupped-hands chat took place at the back of a church hall, after I had preached. Armed with cups of tea and rich tea biscuits, an older couple had approached and asked me 'for a word', which is usually what Phil Mitchell of *EastEnders* says when he's about to kill someone. I feared for my kneecaps.

At first, the couple looked serious and I braced myself at very least for a comment 'shared in love' (some of which I've experienced in the past: they've made me want to flee for safety). I had used storytelling and humour freely during the evening: were they offended? Had my throwaway line about miserable Christians being 'the frozen chosen' who 'knew the Lord but still needed bran' angered them? And I had asked a few provocative questions about theology – not radical enough to

> ⊰⊱
>
> **As the couple came closer, the look in their warm and sparkling eyes set me at ease.**
>
> ⊰

prompt being burnt as a heretic but maybe strong enough to threaten a couple of sacred cows.

As the couple came closer, the look in their warm and sparkling eyes set me at ease. At least, if they were going to complain, they'd be kind. But instead of giving me a good telling-off, they'd come to tell me how much they'd enjoyed the service in general and my preaching in particular. I sighed with relief. Constructive criticism is useful for growth but I don't have to enjoy it. And every once in a while I bump into a stern soul who only begins to look thrilled when they're proving others wrong. Kind words are always much more welcome.

'Jeff, thanks so much for the sermon', the lady whispered. Her husband nodded and chipped in a rhetorical question, in the same hushed tones. 'My, we did have some fun, didn't we?' he said. Did they both fear that the place was bugged? I suddenly realised that both of them were looking around as they spoke, as if they were about to be arrested by the thought police. What was all the secrecy about? Were they about to ask me what Bible version I used and then perhaps offer to sell me cannabis?

'We learned a lot too', said the lady, eager to clarify that they appreciated substance as well as fun. 'It was such a breath of fresh air – it's so nice to enjoy some reality in the church for once.'

We chatted for a few minutes more and as they bade their farewells and walked away I muttered a prayer of thanks for such lovely, thoughtful people who were good enough to stay behind and bring words of strength. But then a couple of questions surfaced and they wouldn't go away. Like the drone of a pair of mosquitoes, they buzzed around between my ears for an hour or so and, months later, they still niggle me.

Why is it that enjoying a belly laugh in church should be so strange and unusual? And if reality is a 'breath of fresh air', then what on earth are these dear folks living on the rest of the time?

Helpfully, we live in a time when the church is increasingly accustomed to public communication that includes humour, storytelling and the preacher being vulnerable rather than projecting an image of being Superman (or woman) minus the blue tights. Yet still there are far too many Christians who find it odd to talk about Monday morning stuff on Sunday mornings without pious or other-worldly language. There are still some churches where a confession of occasional doubt is tantamount to admitting to a dose of herpes and where 'testimonies' always have to have a happy ending. And some Christians can only cope with a faith that always gives the answers but is uncomfortable with lingering questions.

> ❧❧
>
> **I want this book to make you laugh, cry and think, although not necessarily in that order.**
>
> ❧

All of which brings me to this fourth book in the series of my meanderings about life, *Lucas Unleashed*. I fretted initially about the title, because one usually lets dogs off leashes. One *unleashes* a barrage of insults. *Unleashed* sounds perilously close to *unhinged*. It perhaps has the connotations of a madman, out of control. No one wants to read a rant.

With that in mind, let me calm your fears. I want this book to make you laugh, cry and think, although not necessarily in that order. When I complain within these pages, I'll resist the temptation to descend into a lecture and I fully realise that I'm part of the problems that I raise. But *Unleashed* is a good title, because I refuse to get tied up in the straitjacket of protocols, politeness or blandness that can so easily exist in the church.

Perhaps there will be times when I'll say openly in this book what you've been thinking privately. I might express a view that you profoundly disagree with, which is wonderful. We're part of the church, not a cult. Disagreement is part of learning. Either one of us could be wrong. Maybe you'll be provoked to think about something afresh, or embarrass yourself with tears in a public place when you read some of the words that follow. I have a few stunning people to introduce you to in these pages; I still shed tears as I recall them.

But whatever your reaction, I hope that this book unleashes something fresh in you – a hunger for more real talk about faith, a desire for gritty trust that can steer through a whole forest of question marks and perhaps even a deeper love for God and the peculiar people that follow him – us.

And perhaps, who knows? We might have some fun.

With love
Jeff Lucas
Colorado

Serenaded

Last week I was serenaded by three drunk men, which was a first. Their singing wasn't the greatest, mainly because one of the trio took an independent pathway and sang in a different key. His timing was well out too; he was at least a second behind with the lyrics. He sounded like a discordant echo.

The experience took place during a karaoke event. I'm highly averse to karaoke, (which is probably a Japanese word meaning 'tone deaf') because it usually showcases the talents of people who shouldn't sing in the shower, never mind in public. Despite all this, the song that the merry triumvirate warbled so tunelessly was a very sweet sound indeed.

It happened during a national ministers' conference and, fear not, the chaps who had been too long at the wine were not part of the clerical gathering. Two thousand pastors had descended on a convention centre in San Diego. I was one of the conference speakers; Kay, my wife, was with me and we decided to pop to the hotel bar late one evening for a nightcap. There were a few pastors from the conference scattered around the bar; some engaged in earnest conversations about life, church and the universe.

I noticed that most were sipping lemonade. Emboldened by the opening miracle of John's gospel, we ordered a couple of glasses of Cabernet Sauvignon.

Enter the loud and lubricated threesome. They were not so much drunk as buoyant after a boozy night out and were celebrating a forthcoming wedding. They ordered drinks and then turned to greet us as though we were old friends. They were intrigued by our English accents and happily told us all about their evening, their lives, jobs and a host of other details. One even asked Kay why such a beautiful lady had decided to marry an elderly man like me.

> ⋲⋲
>
> **I was worn out by the 'tyranny of the oughts' that often stalks me.**
>
> ⋲

We chatted for a while and they seemed to like us. At one point one apologised for their being in such high spirits and said that if we wanted them to go away, they'd be happy to, as they didn't want to be a bother. We encouraged them to stay, as we were enjoying ourselves. The leadership conference had meant that we had spent a couple of enjoyable but furrow-browed days trying to figure out how we could change the world more efficiently. I was worn out by the 'tyranny of the oughts' that often stalks me at Christian gatherings and just a little impatient with the Christian church that, despite being called to radical change, often squeals when we change the hymn books. A bit of non-churchy chat was refreshing, even if it was with chaps who slurred their words.

At last I finally confessed to being a minister and a public speaker. I thought they might instantly sober up, put garlic around their necks, or flee: not everyone likes ministers. But if they were alarmed at the presence of a cleric, they didn't show it, which is good since there were a couple of thousand nearby. The best-man-to-be among them asked for some tips for his wedding speech, which I gladly helped with.

And then it happened. They excused themselves, went over to the dreaded karaoke machine and signed up to do a turn. Minutes later, before launching into an almost unrecognisable version of an Elton John classic, one of them made the surprising dedication. He pointed haphazardly in our direction:

'We'd like to dedicate this song to our friends over there, Jeff and Kay Lucas . . . This one's for you.' I felt the eyes of some of the earnest, lemonade-sipping clergy in the place fix onto me – or was it my imagination? I stared straight ahead, wondering if people would think I'd been out on the razzle and had teamed up with an inebriated gaggle of wannabe lounge singers . . .

And then I smiled, grateful that the happy threesome wanted to be with us. They didn't run when I said I was a minister. Without making too much of the moment, it taught me a lesson.

I'd like to be someone that people who don't know God want to be around. That doesn't mean that my life should never present a challenge to them; we're called to be the salt of the earth, not sugar. I'm not suggesting that we adopt a bland compliance, looking and sounding exactly like everyone else because we want to fit in. Sometimes the choices we make and the stands we take will challenge those who don't want to follow Christ.

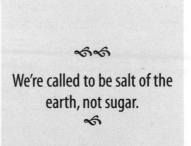

⤳⤳

We're called to be salt of the earth, not sugar.

⤳

But the song dedication and the chat that night nudge me to pray that God will make me winsome enough to receive some unexpected invitations, which is what happened to Jesus. But that's always risky; hanging out with the unholy meant that he was constantly misunderstood by the religious. Yet he wouldn't back off and was determined to spend time with the 'wrong' crowd, who loved him, not just because of his legendary capacity for providing great wine at parties. In his culture, having a drink or a meal with someone was far more than a casual act: it spoke of acceptance and identification. The miracle was not only that Jesus wanted to spend time with sinners but that *they* wanted to spend time with *him*. The antithesis of the poker-faced Pharisees, who shunned die-hard sinners, Jesus welcomed them. And they rolled out the red carpet for him in return.

Those who follow him are supposed to be like him. Being like him means taking the same risks.

A human sunset

I've missed too many sunsets.

Travel, my schedule and my relentless commitment to hurtling breathlessly through most of my days means that I have missed so many appointments with the setting sun. A self-confessed quickaholic, it seems to me that in an idyllic existence, we would all pause at each day's end: to be grateful, to clink glasses in a toast, to lift our hearts in heartfelt worship not of the sun but of the One who created it. Sadly, too often the nightly performance in the sky plays itself out but I don't make it to the show. Annie Dillard, calling us to be people who notice, laments that 'all too often creation plays to an empty house.'

But not today. A late afternoon walk in the country treated us to an absolutely stunning sunset. It demanded our rapt attention. Our walk was suspended for a while; it would have been wrong not to just stand still and

෧෧

'all too often creation plays to an empty house.'

෧

gaze. Lurid oranges tinged with blood red tangerines silently mushroomed across the dimming sky, gradually swallowing up the dusky blues and browns. Previously stark outlines of great trees melted and finally disappeared into hillsides, as, at last, the sun sank and God signed off another day with an extravagant flourish. It was a perfect ending. Dallas Willard says that God is always at play throughout the earth. This light show in the sky was a masterpiece, of even greater value because it was gone seconds later. God's art is usually for the moment, not for the museum. And that makes it easy to miss.

But yesterday I met a human being in their sunset and it was an equally breathtaking sight. James came up for a chat at the end of a service where I had been the speaker. An elderly man with snow white hair and bright, gentle eyes, he was brimming with kindness and apparently carefree. Nothing could be further from the truth. I didn't know then that James was living on Death Row.

Later, James's son approached me and asked if I would be willing to take a moment to pray with his dad. The three of us stood together and I asked how I might best pray. 'Dad's got terminal cancer and he's been told that he's not got long. That's right, isn't it Dad?' I winced inwardly, nervous about this stark acknowledgement of a death sentence: but then I settled, aware that this family were facing the ugliest news head on. 'Dad's in constant agony: right now he is in unbearable pain.' I looked again into James's eyes: they gave no hint of the screaming torture that he was enduring. 'I'm so sorry to trouble you' said James, concerned. 'It won't take a minute, will it?' I wanted to tell him that if it took a day or a week, it would be fine. If we could just pray him out of his searing pain, whatever the end result of our asking, it would be an honour to pray with him. Why is it that some of those who suffer so greatly are reluctant to place the slightest imposition on others?

I placed my hands on both of them and then the trouble began. I wanted to pray with solemn authority, insisting that every trace of cancer be driven from his body, right now. I wanted so much to declare James free of every mutant cell, so that he could live to see his grandchildren live long. But I couldn't. Over the years, I've offered my *amens* to lots of prayers that insisted that cancer be evicted but to no avail. I still utterly believe that God is able and that he still heals people, somewhere, sometimes, today. A doctor friend prayed for a chap with incurable cancer – with a number of secondary tumours. The survival rate for that cancer beyond two years is less than 5%. Some six years later, the patient is still very much alive, enjoying a perfectly healthy life. But my own confidence in healing prayer has been dented. I struggle to know what to ask for and I've heard too many preachers deride healing prayers that include the phrase 'if it is your will' as woolly faithlessness (even though Jesus taught us to say those very words in what we call the Lord's Prayer).

I asked that God's grace would hold James and his family, that divine intervention would come, however it came. A few minutes later, I said goodbye to James, hoping it was not a final farewell. Out in the car park, his son thanked me profusely for the gift of a few seconds. It is I who needed to thank him: humanly speaking, I have more time on my hands than his dad. But he was so grateful and kind: like father, like son.

❧❧

A few minutes later, I said goodbye to James, hoping it was not a final farewell.

❧

In the car moments later, I realised that I had just witnessed one of life's wonders: a man, in his sunset moments, at peace and dying well. I'd very much like James to recover and for God, the big G, to get credit for being bigger than the big C. But if cancer takes him, even soon, it will not have won, for this sunset will not end in total dusk. The light of hope and faith, the light that is Jesus, the resurrection and the life, will not be overwhelmed even by death itself.

You are a beautiful sunset, James. I'm so glad I didn't miss you.

Batman

I think I'm turning into a bat. The metamorphosis is quite advanced. It's worrying that I hang upside down daily, because of the recent acquisition of a new piece of gym equipment. My last birthday included the number 5 and I've been getting promotional letters from the American Association for Retired People, which means that I can get great deals on dentures and cut price tickets for coach trips to the seaside.

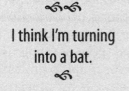

I think I'm turning into a bat.

My smiling wife has offered to knit me a blanket to keep my knees warm.

And so, in frantic search of youth, I bought something called an *inverter*. This strange piece of machinery looks like an instrument of torture, which is what it is. Clamped firmly into it, the machine flips me upside down, stretching out my vertebrae and dumping every ounce of blood into my head. I look flushed crimson with embarrassment for hours. Extremely overweight people should not attempt this upside down move: suffering concussion from being slapped soundly in the head by your own belly is not fun. Kay also inverts daily, because the family that hangs upside down together stays together. It's all very batlike. It's apparently good for us to hang so daily, although I have yet to be convinced. None of the handy accessories that come with being a bat are showing up in my life, like radar, night vision, or the ability to spot a tasty mouse snack from five hundred feet.

But the main reason for my worry about turning into an *eptesicus fuscus* (the posh Latin name for a bat) is my discovery that bats spend their lives yelling. It's how they do life. It's all to do with their built-in navigational system. I used to think of the diminutive bat as being as blind, as, you guessed it, a bat. Extensive research (five minutes on the internet) reveals that this is just an urban myth, like the ridiculous notions that Elvis is alive and living in Birmingham, or that the overhead projector is a great invention. Bats actually have keen eyesight – but they do rely on something called *echo location* in order to live. Echo location enables a bat to emit high frequency sound waves that bounce off an object, such as a passing mosquito, to produce a type of sound 'echo' that returns to the bat's ears. In short, bats get through life by yelling. That's how the little critter makes sense of his existence – by non-stop yelling and by measuring the world's response to his yells.

So bats spend all their lives yelling. They yell at each other, they yell at their lunch, they yell at the trees, they yell at their neighbours and they yell at their babies. They're born yelling and they die yelling and when they're really on a roll, they can yell up to two hundred times a second. Most of their yelling is inaudible to the human ears, for which we must be grateful.

And this is where I come in.

I don't actually *yell* much, at least out loud. But I have discovered that I can spend too much of my life yelling within, out of earshot of others. I can live with a simmering irritation, a silent shout that is the emotional equivalent of a kettle forever close to the boil. I allow my evening to be wrecked by that most British of traditions, bad service in restaurants, and instead of laughing at the Fawlty Towers ineptitude, I bristle. I mutter about the price of petrol, find myself seething about the bunged up car park that is the M25 and tut-tut at the pathetic triviality of a culture that is even vaguely interested in the Big Brother house. I'm irritated by the worship

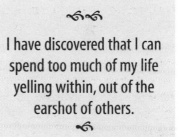

∽∽

I have discovered that I can spend too much of my life yelling within, out of the earshot of others.

∽

song that insists I declare that I'm ecstatic during every waking moment because of Jesus and nurse violent thoughts about that strange person on the train who has a Barry Manilow ring tone on their phone. All these conspire to keep me inwardly yelling; thus gratitude is replaced by an ongoing internal rant that simmers just beneath my skin.

And there are some people who take all this fuming to the next step and spend every waking moment of their lives literally yelling. Complaining is their forte, they're not happy unless they're not happy and they forever test others to see what reaction they can get to their shouts. Rage is what they do best, so each day is another series of encounters where they get on people's nerves, wind them up and put them down.

What a life – seeing everything upside down, mostly in the dark, yelling and usually parked very close to a pile of bat poo. Great for *eptesicus fuscus*.

Bad for *homo sapiens*.

Swinging the sword of truth

Today I witnessed some tragic Bible bashing. America has been gripped by the trial of serial killer Dennis Rader, who tortured and murdered ten victims over a thirty-year period. 'Monster' is an overused word in criminal cases but this chilling man fits the bill. He was sentenced to 145 years in prison and he will not be eligible for parole for forty years. What compounds the tragedy is that he describes himself as a Christian and until recently was president of a Lutheran congregation. In a rambling statement, he quoted from the Bible, read a few lines from a daily devotional book and suggested that his three-decade killing spree was inspired by demons. He thanked his defence team with the gushing gratitude of an Oscar winner. But not once did he ever pause to make a serious, considered apology to the relatives of his victims. The best he could manage was, 'As for remorse, well, that's obvious.' But it wasn't. Sorry would have been a small but welcome start.

The American court system permits the relatives of victims to make a statement at sentence hearings; fifteen individuals decided to speak up. As this trial was being held in America's Bible belt, most of them were professing

Christians. And in most cases, their hatred for Rader was palpable. Through gritted teeth, they told him that he would burn in hell forever. Some were obviously thrilled at the prospect. The most vitriolic statement came from a man who had written a Christian book on suffering. He rained down insults on the killer of his mother with glee and pro- nounced yet another 'You'll roast forever without pos- sibility of parole' sent- ence. There was something obscene about the relish with which he spoke the words, his face twisted with rage. For a second, it seemed like there was more than one monster in the courtroom. 'Hell will freeze over before I forgive', he told reporters later.

∽∽

The most vitriolic statement came from a man who had written a Christian book on suffering.

∾

I don't want to judge the relatives of those victims. I cannot imagine their agony, or begin to fathom the depths of their grief. As I listened to the grisly catalogue of crimes, I found myself shouting at the television. Rader is certainly a loathsome specimen and I have no idea how I would react if he had snuffed out the life of my son or daughter: I fear I might join those baying for his barbecuing. None of us know how we would respond if tested and we all fervently pray that we will never sit that particular exam.

But tragedy begets tragedy and today's event lacked all hope, because not one of these professed followers of Christ – perpetrator or victims – could find grace to seek or offer the beginnings of forgiveness. Justice must be done and Rader must never see the light of day in a com- munity again; but yesterday, both the condemned and the condemners slopped around in the same sad pool of sin. And the Bible was used by both sides, as it has been so many times throughout history, like a clumsily swung sword, slicing not only those in the actual courtroom but anyone who watched the proceeding on TV. The Bible is a dangerous weapon in the wrong hands.

I couldn't help wondering if the victims' families were committing themselves to ongoing life sentences behind the invisible yet nonetheless iron bars of bitterness. Rage is not a laser-focussed missile – it blows up in our own faces. The first person to benefit from forgiving is the forgiver; it is not only an act of stunning generosity that extends to others but a canny strategy for self-preservation. Forgiveness literally is the gift that keeps on giving, most of all to the one who gives it away.

> ∽∾
> **Truth sometimes hurts but am I occasionally hurtful in the way I share it?**
> ∾

So I'm profoundly challenged not only about my own capacity to bestow forgiveness but also the way in which I use Scripture. Truth sometimes hurts but am I occasionally hurtful in the way I share it? Too many Christians have sliced and diced each other in the name of Christ. We can be so intent on applying the serrated edge of Scripture that we forget that the truth without love is no truth at all.

And hell, whatever that is, will not freeze over. But heaven still stands on tiptoe, waiting in hopeful anticipation for the walking wounded ones who limp on, still bloodied, yet refusing to resort to biblical bludgeoning and beginning to forgive.

Welcome

We just recently moved our UK home to a little village that nestles in the lovely green hills of the South Downs. At times it feels that we have stepped into an Agatha Christie novel, minus the murders, so quaint and quintessentially English is the place. There's a pub that serves heavenly food, a post office that opens infrequently and an unmanned farm shop: you take what you need, write your name in a book and leave the money in a bowl. This is an enterprise based on a rare commodity these days: trust. It's wonderful. Just a mile from the South Downs Way, I'm able to run my four-mile session of agony while looking down at the patchwork quilt that is the gorgeous countryside below.

> ❧❧
>
> There's a pub that serves heavenly food, a post office that opens infrequently and an unmanned farm shop.
>
> ❧

But we wondered whether we would fit into this community. Some people around these parts have had family connections locally for over a hundred years: what would they make of newcomers? And then most people in the village speak with a plummy accent that makes me feel, Essex male that I am, like Del Boy at a gymkhana. Chatting with a sixteen-year-old lad in the village the other day, I was expecting to have to natter away about *I'm a celebrity, get me out of here*, the latest from Eminem, or how Arsenal were doing in the Cup. Knowing that I was new, he asked, in yet another Oxbridge accent, if I had seen the inside of Arundel Cathedral. I replied that I had not. 'Oh, you absolutely must', he exclaimed. 'It's really quite exquisite.' I fled, shamed by this culturally aware adolescent.

But we got a glorious shock when we actually moved in. One of our neighbours showed up with a bottle of champagne and then announced that she had planned a welcome party for us. A few weeks later, we were the honoured guests at a beautifully catered 'do', where yet more champagne flowed freely. Quite a few people came, including the local vicar and his wife; he is a smiling, kind man, who told me, without out a hint of frostiness, that he and I 'come from

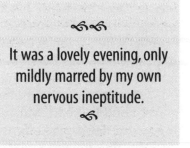

❧❧

It was a lovely evening, only mildly marred by my own nervous ineptitude.

❧

different ends of the candle.' Having visited the church, to say that it is 'high' is a bit like saying that Everest is a bit big. This bloke blesses everything that moves, chants all his prayers and ceremonially lobs water around like a Baptist on Duracells. But despite our different 'churchpersonship' I deeply appreciate his warmth and am inspired and challenged by his obvious love for God.

We asked our most marvellous, party-throwing neighbour why she had been so generous and she said that she simply wanted to make us feel welcome. It was a lovely evening, only mildly marred by my own nervous ineptitude. Everybody there spoke in such upper class tones. An hour or so into it, I found myself emulating them. Gone was the lad from Ilford, enter 'Enry 'Iggins from Windsor; Eton actually. My pronunciation of the word 'house' – (usually, 'ouse') turned miraculously to 'hice.' Horrors! I was turning into Prince Charles, I thought, nervously checking the size of my ears.

The kindness has continued. We went to the Village Hall to see the local amateur dramatics society perform a whodunit. We walked in nervously, desperately hoping to spot some familiar faces. Within a few seconds, Ian the farmer (he owns the 'on your honour' farm shop), rushed over to us, a huge smile taking over his whole face, his hand extended warmly. Seeming genuinely delighted to meet us, Ian insisted that we join him and his wife for the evening. He told us about pasteurising milk, how his barn had mysteriously burned down and his plans for the future . . .

. . . and made us feel utterly at home.

Yet another heart-warming, if not mildly embarrassing, event took place in another local pub at the other end of the village, next to the railway station. I'd returned from a day in London and tried to start the car that I'd left in the station car park, to no avail. The battery was dead. I called the rescue services, was told that someone with mechanical skills would be at my side within a month or so (okay, two hours) and so I settled into the pub for a meal. A couple of chaps from the village wandered over, beer in hand, keen for a chat. Asking me where I lived, I said that I too was from the village and named the place where we have an apartment.

Their eyes widened with interest. 'We hear that a couple have moved in there who spend quite a lot of their time in America. Apparently he is a writer and is fairly well known in his field. They come and go quite quietly. Have you bumped into them yet?'

To my horror, I realised that I was the chap they were talking about. I spend a lot of time in the USA. Half my life is spent writing these days. And as for the famous bit, I suppose that I'm relatively well known in the British church scene. I gulped. 'I think that's me you're talking about.'

> ᦥᦥ
>
> **Apparently he is a writer and is fairly well known in his field.**
>
> ᦥ

They flushed with crimson-faced embarrassment and one of them swore. But despite the little gaffe, our time together in the pub was warm and fun. They'd lived in the community for over a hundred years between them – but still made me feel right at home.

All of which made me wonder about church. Often we ask deep and searching questions about what church should and shouldn't be. We theologise and theorise and rightly consider our methodology and how we can more effectively communicate our message. All of which matters – but doesn't matter at all, if we're a cold, difficult cliquey crowd who sniff at newcomers, fuss them away from our pews and make it tough for them to belong. Generosity, giving nervous newcomers a smile of welcome – and our seats – none of this is rocket science but it can make all the difference. Without basic kindness, visitors will only ever darken the doors of our church buildings once. They might be moved by the message but alienated by us. So let's be welcoming.

Got to go. I absolutely must see the inside of Arundel Cathedral. I hear that it's really quite exquisite . . .

Taxi

The glowing orange light atop the black London cab signalled that it was available for hire. The sight of it warmed my heart, a welcome beacon at the end of a long day. Cold and bone-weary, I was eager to catch the next train home. And then, as the taxi pulled over to the pavement in response to my wave, I saw the pennant.

A huge triangular banner was dangling from the cabbie's rear view mirror, filling the centre of his windscreen. It was made

> ❧❧
>
> The scarlet and gold combination together produced a colourful scream: *JESUS NEVER FAILS!*
>
> ❧

from crimson velvet and boasted garish gold lettering. The scarlet and gold combination together produced a colourful scream: *JESUS NEVER FAILS!*

As I climbed into the cab, my thoughts were mixed. I was glad to meet another Christian but felt slightly concerned about his choice of cab decoration – which then made me feel guilty for being worried. With its frilly gold trim, I imagined that this in-your-face piece of evangelistic merchandise had been purchased at a Christian bookshop during the seventies, the decade of tastelessness. Or perhaps the cabbie had persuaded his mother to sacrifice her curtains for the sake of the gospel.

Slamming the door shut and taking my seat, I tapped on the glass window that separated me from the driver. He turned and beamed a huge grin, seemingly thrilled to see me. I was just another unknown passenger but he welcomed me like a king. Immediately, the pennant made sense. His laughter-lined face banished any fear that he was a sombre zealot on a mission to make the good news sound bad. I relaxed.

'Victoria Station, please' I said and then added, pointing to the banner, 'It's true, isn't it, about Jesus? He never fails.'

The driver's face widened into an even broader smile. 'Do you know him?' he asked: not an interrogation but a delighted enquiry. I affirmed that, yes, I did know Jesus. He greeted me like a long lost brother and then told me the reason for the banner. Nine out of ten people who ride with him make a comment about his velvet accessory. It's a talking point, a way to introduce God into the day. I wasn't surprised to hear that the pennant launches so many chats. It's big enough to eclipse the sun. He even had a little collection of tracts on hand to give away to people who wanted to know more. I marvelled. This was a man who was at ease in his own skin; there was nothing forced or aggressive about him. He had simply found Jesus to be wonderfully trustworthy and wanted the world to know it.

∾∽

'This ride is to bless you', he insisted.

∾

22

All too soon, we pulled up outside Victoria Station. He steadfastly refused my payment: 'This ride is to bless you', he insisted. I squirmed with the embarrassment peculiar to adults confronted with a random act of kindness. As I walked into the bustling station, I wondered. Twenty-five years ago I had thrown away the gigantic yellow 'Jesus never fails' sticker that had bedecked my own car. My motor has been fishless for decades. I decided quite a long while ago to abandon my badges and lapel pins, insisting that a cheesy slogan or a King James Version Scripture text T-shirt was unlikely to prompt the masses to hysterical conversion. I am no longer a walking evangelistic billboard.

But the smiling, joyful, generous cabbie challenged me not to grab a badge or sport a sticker but simply to be willing to be more open about God. How desperately he is needed in our rapidly unravelling world. And I asked myself: have I become so laid back about God that I am in danger of never talking about him?

Having missed my train, I parked myself in a station bar and soon found myself in conversation with a high-flying city type. Before long, that conversation naturally moved to the subject of God. I was a little bolder than usual about my faith. Later, I meandered down to the platform, still tired, yet strangely refreshed; grateful for a moment to talk about Christ; thankful for a taxi driver who inspired me to be bold.

It's true, isn't it? Jesus never fails. However we share it, it's the message that's worth sharing. But sometimes, as the next piece shows, we might need to think about what *sharing* means . . .

Silent witness?

It had been a good flight. The nine hour transatlantic trek had been spent eating food that surprisingly looked and tasted like food; I had managed to spend a good amount of time tapping at my laptop and I was feeling the warm glow of productivity. And the chap next to me had been friendly but not verbose. We'd had a few little chats during the journey but he had spent much of his time sleeping, blanket pulled up around his ears and sporting an eye mask that made him look like he was next in line for a firing squad. Absentmindedly, I listened to the singer on my iPod, (Ronan Keating, in case you're interested), assuring me that I was at my best, communication-wise, when I say 'nothing at all'. Was he really saying that true beauty can be discovered in silence? Or that there are some people who should just shut up?

> ⋙⋘
>
> At no point did he ever ask me what I did, for which I was glad.
>
> ⋘

An hour from Heathrow, it was time for breakfast. My fellow passenger blinked his way into consciousness and, seeing that I was no longer working, launched into another session of pleasant chatter. We talked about the financial markets (depressing), the Saturday night binge drinking culture of Britain (even more depressing) and he told me a little about the few days of business that he was about to do in London. At no point did he ever ask me what I did, for which I was glad. Too many warm conversations with strangers have ended abruptly when we got to the part when I say that I'm a minister. I didn't want him to clam his lips tight, replace his eye mask and request that he be shot, or even worse, make a beeline for the emergency exit. I'm not at all ashamed of Jesus, in case you were wondering. But I don't like the image that Christians sometimes project: bumbling, irrelevant clerics; ranting crowds outside an abortion clinic, baying for blood even as they insist on its value; other-worldly characteristics that make it appear that we are newly landed from Jupiter; dull church activities where hordes are miraculously healed from insomnia. For these reasons and more, I am reluctant to take the label 'Christian' without at least qualifying what I mean by wearing it.

At last, my businessman friend turned to me, looked into my eyes and I thought we had reached the point when he would enquire about my occupation. But we had not. On the contrary.

'I've enjoyed sitting next to you Jeff. I keep finding myself parked next to effing evangelicals' (to be clear, he didn't actually say *effing*). 'They're so weird that I get endless material for dinner party conversation from them.' As I listened with horror, he told me about a couple of keen Christian chaps who had assaulted him with 'good news' during a recent flight, insisting that the Lord had choreographed the seating arrangements They had even held an impromptu prayer meeting on the plane, while he silently fumed. But there was nothing silent about him now. Angry vitriol flowed from his lips; this man despised all things Christian.

Now I was in a moral dilemma. My natural inclination was to tell him, calmly and quietly, that not only was I one of those effing, I mean evangelicals but that I was a minister to boot. As he ranted on, I felt the need to own up, to admit my identity. And then the thought struck me: why was I about to break cover? Was it for me to feel better about myself, or was it to help him? I'd felt accomplished about my laptop work – now did I want to feel evangelistically productive too?

With just minutes before landing now, I knew that if I spoke up, he would be paralysed by embarrassment. He'd apologise until we landed and I'd have no time to reassure him. I would feel that I had been heroic, flashing my Christian identity card in his face – and he would feel shamed. Nonetheless, I did feel mildly Judas-like as I sat there, quietly listening to yet another tale of zealous Christian insanity.

And then there was the additional problem: I partially agreed with some of his complaints. Having been one of those Christians who treated evangelism as a monologue and who used to go on the hunt for 'souls' with the passion of an Apache with a pair of garden shears, I agreed with much of what he said. Now I was really confused – would an admission that I was a Christian enable me to apologise for the over-enthusiastic behaviour of some of my Christian family members?

This is the moment in this story where you wonder: so what happened next? I'd like you to know that I announced, gently, that I was a Christian. I sympathised with his anger and didn't blame him for his prejudices. His eyes brimmed over with tears as I told him that

Jesus was wonderful and that he had a plan for his life. I'd like you to know all of that, because that's how these stories are supposed to end, or so we think. The now redeemed businessman leaves the plane with a new spring in his step, clutching the piece of evangelistic literature which I always carry for emergencies (or opportunities) and promising to call me to let me know how the Alpha course was going . . .

But none of that is true. What actually happened is that nothing happened. I prayed like mad that he would ask me what I did – and decided that this question would be a green light from God that I should break cover. I pondered in my mind how I could best let him off the hook and walk away from our conversation with something positive. But he never did ask. And so I didn't say anything.

We parted with a warm handshake and a smile. Even now, days later, I'm not sure if I did the right thing. Was my sitting next to him a golden opportunity missed, a chance to put the record straight, that I squandered? Or was my silence a greater act of human kindness?

Perhaps one day he'll stumble over a book of mine, or a website, and

∽∽

Right or wrong, I'll leave it to God.

∽

realise and remember that he was deriding those hated Christians to one of their own. Or maybe he doesn't have to do any of that; perhaps this is a lesson to me, that my opening my mouth is not the only way that people are reached.

Right or wrong, I'll leave it to God. But this is certain: when I do open my mouth to talk about Jesus, I want to

27

represent him with the same warmth, sensitivity and kindness that he consistently showed when on earth. And maybe, just maybe, sometimes love might be best expressed by us saying nothing at all.

Celebrating the ordinary

Some Christians give the impression that the Christian life is like living in Disneyland. They apparently skip from one breathless roller-coaster experience of God to another. The Lord seems to be very, very busily engaged in almost constant conversation with them, they enjoy a broadband prayer life and epic miracles accompany their every waking hour. Bluntly, I don't find the life of faith to be like this. God is wonderful and my life has been punctuated with more than my fair share of wonders but many of my days fade into grey and should be filed under the heading of 'nothing much happened.'

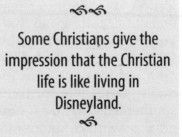

Some Christians give the impression that the Christian life is like living in Disneyland.

But perhaps we should look at those lack-lustre days with renewed appreciation. I write this from sweltering Banda Aceh, Indonesia, the city that suffered the greatest losses from the Boxing Day earthquake and tsunami that followed in 2004. On that day, something extraordinary happened to the sea, which bunched itself into a wave that delivered a knock-out punch to the town. Over two hundred thousand people perished here in that pummelling, including the inhabitants of a coastal fishing village that disappeared in seconds. Tired fishermen pointed their boats back towards port and home that night, unaware that a monster had crept beneath their bows while they fussed over their nets. To their horror, there was no port; no homes to sleep in and no wives and children to greet them. All were gone.

This morning I sipped coffee with Wahuel, a delightful smiling man who told me that I looked young from the neck down (almost a compliment). Wahuel had lost both his children to that wicked wave. His wife's entire family had been wiped out. And yesterday I chatted with a giggling Nurlaila, a delightful fifteen-year-old whose home is still the temporary barracks that were hastily thrown up in the wake of that terrible day. Both her parents perished; and just seconds after telling me that, she burst into singing – in perfect English – the Abba classic *I Have A Dream* – with its line about believing in angels. I'm sure she does but for a moment I wondered how. There are so many here whose lives have been smashed to smithereens by that ominously historic day. Mass graves abound, anonymous resting places for thousands: many were never found, swallowed up by the ravenous beast that was the sea.

All of which makes a restoration of relative normality a delight to behold. We've visited the Community and Children's Centre run by Children on the Edge, the charity originally launched by Body Shop founder, the late Anita Roddick. It's a hive of bustling ordinariness. Kindergarten children giggle on the swings. Computer skills classes are held in one room; embroidery in another. In the large hall, a children's choir practise their performance for an upcoming concert. All very ordinary and wonderful with it.

Last night, we attended a football match organised by Children on the Edge, the culmination of a two week tournament. It was just like an England World Cup match – a mixture of brilliance and ineptitude, a penalty shoot out nail-biter to decide the result and even a petulant young Rooney wannabe given a red card and sent off for fouling and then getting lippy with the ref. We cheered ourselves hoarse as the grinning captain held the moulded plastic trophy aloft, which was almost as big as him. The goalkeeper was the hero/saviour and so was thrown up into the air in celebration.

I wiped a tear away as I watched ordinary kids enjoying another ordinary day: free from fear, for a moment at least, of a monster wave; able to dream about bending it like Beckham, to laugh and argue and pull faces and have melting ice cream running down their chins; able to do what kids do best, living extravagantly for the moment. These people don't want a life that looks like a disaster movie but where the special effects are real; they'd just like to laugh and cry, wake and sleep, love and die like everybody else.

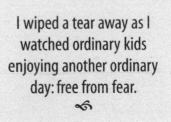

~~

I wiped a tear away as I watched ordinary kids enjoying another ordinary day: free from fear.

~

Perhaps you are suffering from the disease that can afflict those who know for sure where their next meal is coming from – boredom. The ordinary looks dull. Be grateful for those days of quiet predictability, where nothing much happens, including nothing much that is bad. Somehow, the ordinary can start to look magnificent.

For more information about Children on the Edge, check out www.childrenontheedge.org

Change

I've decided that the older I get, the more I become a creature of habit. I like tea in the morning, coffee in the afternoon and anything made with grapes at night. I've developed habits that make frequent flying, preaching, writing and much of the rest of my life a little easier. Good habits can be helpful.

But I take some of my habits to ridiculous extremes. I used to wear contact lenses – I've given them up now because I'm reluctant to poke myself in the eyes on a daily basis. But I had developed a nice little routine for their insertion. I'd always put the left lens in first and then the right. Left. Right. No deviation. This meant that I would never confuse the two, which is helpful, as my prescription differs so much for each eye. If I get them mixed up, I end up seeing a world that looks like what you see in a hall of bendy mirrors.

One morning, I mistakenly placed the right lens into my right eye first.

> ❧❧
>
> My addiction to ritual was seriously messed up last week when we moved house.
>
> ❧

33

There was no sin in this, nor health risk: the universe was not about to explode. But it all seemed wrong. I am sad to say that I removed the right lens, replaced it in the contact lens holder, placed the left lens in my left eye and then replaced the right lens in my right eye. I need therapy.

My addiction to ritual was seriously messed up last week when we moved house. If you are considering doing this, my advice is – don't. Given a choice between moving again and being immersed upside down in a vat of hot fat, I think I'd take the latter. They say that moving is stressful: our marriage did fairly well as our lives were stuffed into boxes. Besides which, being Christians, we don't argue. We just share intensely.

But the move showed me how much I like what once has been. I struggled to part with some items which I've never used and never will. We have souvenirs from long gone holidays that only clutter up our kitchen drawers. Occasionally we will view them with nostalgia.

I'm not alone in my love of sameness. Most churches don't do well with change. I'm not declaring war on *tradition* here, which has great value. It's quite traditional to wash. Be old-fashioned and bathe daily. Your friends will thank you for it. But *traditionalism* can be a curse that chokes all possibility of life and change. Some people think that rearranging the chairs or pews in the church building is a worse crime than denying the doctrine of justification by faith. A church in America is currently having a three way split over the location of a piano stool (I'm serious about this – how I wish I was joking).

Perhaps the most bizarre example of the struggle to change that I've met, comes from a member of the Salvation Army who recently wrote to me. At a time when the Army is asking questions of itself about being more effective and relevant in today's world, not everyone is finding change easy. The specific issue the letter covered was a waste bin in the corps ladies' toilets. There are now two bins for used hand towels. One is a small pedal type which has been of good

> ❦❦
>
> **Change comes hard, even when it is for the better.**
> ❦

service for some time and the other a new larger flip top bin.

Someone asked why there were two bins in the ladies' toilets. The answer shows a thoughtful leadership strategy – and a snail's approach to the new. 'We are changing to the big bin but we wanted to give people time to get used to it before removing the old one.' Apparently there was a fear that the sisters of the church might experience trauma if their beloved (if a little overful) small bin was removed too quickly. News of this made me want to call the Samaritans.

Change comes hard, even when it is for the better. And we often complicate the process more because we insist that *our* preferences are *God's* preferences. Now it's not just that we are offended: God is too.

Let it be known concerning the layout of pews, the bins in the bathroom, the order of insertion of contact lenses, the position of the church piano, the time we meet on Sundays and a host of other minutiae: God isn't nervous or worried. He is highly concerned about a planet staggering on without knowledge of his love; he does get upset and moved by children who are used by vile traffickers as sexual cargo. There is a stirring in his heart when we recklessly plunder the planet as if we owned it, when in fact he only ever gave it to us on temporary loan. Most of the other things that cause our small minds to worry and our small hearts to flutter don't bother him at all, including the bins.

There's a postscript to this story.

This epic saga of the bins is such a graphic illustration of our capacity for pettiness, that I decided to tell it during a sermon about change. I finished preaching, the service ended and a man made a beeline for me. I knew that I was in big trouble. The look on his face suggested that he wanted me dead.

'I am really upset with you', he snapped. I immediately went into apologetic mode, without knowing the reason for his wanting me not to benefit from having a pulse. 'I'm so sorry', I stammered, frantically rewinding the sermon in my head to locate the source of the problem.

'I'm from the church with the bins', he barked. Ah. So that's it. Beam me up, Scotty.

'And today, Jeff, you mocked our church.' Self-observation over the years has taught me that, for whatever reason, be it noble or self-preservation, always apologise in full – even if I have little or nothing to be sorry for. So I began a contrite speech, begging his forgiveness, regretting sincerely that I had offended him. He cut me off. It was to get worse.

'I'll have you know that the small bin – the bin you mocked (here he seemed to wipe away a tear) was given in memory of my beloved grandmother.' Yikes. This was a memorial bin. Now I knew I was in trouble up to my neck. There was still worse news to come: 'Granny died just a few weeks ago. So when you performed your little routine up on that platform today, you mocked our church and insulted the precious memory of our dear granny.' If I had been thinking clearly, instead of concentrating on grovelling, I might have wondered how a bin that had been in the church for decades could be a memorial to a granny who only just departed . . . but my mind was otherwise occupied.

I decided that if a local sackcloth and ashes store – Repentance 'R' us – was nearby – I'd rush to it immediately and put a full set of remorse kit on. I could spend the rest of the conference walking around whimpering, 'Woe is me', while whipping myself in a most holy fashion. I could carry a sign that read, 'My name is Jeff and I am a loud-mouthed, insensitive scumbag. Even your granny isn't safe when I'm in town.' But I sensed that even such extreme acts of contrition would not be enough for my enraged accuser. For five terrible minutes, I apologised, pleaded, grovelled and even cried.

Of course, in the back of my head, I was having second thoughts. What kind of bizarrely dysfunctional family decides to donate a waste-paper bin for the ladies loo when Granny pops her clogs? Could this perhaps begin a new tradition in the church? We could have the Jeffrey R. Lucas Memorial Toilet Brush when I finally shuffle off this mortal coil (Yes, every time we use that brush, we remember his hairstyle with fondness . . .) but I didn't share these

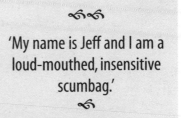

᪥᪥

'My name is Jeff and I am a loud-mouthed, insensitive scumbag.'

᪥

thoughts. My wannabe executioner was already irate; to suggest that his family was odd wouldn't help. So I just kept on saying how sorry I was, which wasn't hard, because, however weird his story was, I don't want to hurt anyone.

After what seemed forever, there was a pause in my begging and, suddenly, the expression on his face changed and he winked.

'I'm joking, Jeff', he smiled.

What?

'I'm just joking. I thought it might be fun to pull your leg. I'm not from that church. It's just a joke.'

Ever felt a mixture of totally contradictory feelings? I want to hug him and hit him, to celebrate because I was not an insensitive windbag and be furious because he had strapped me in an emotional torture chamber.

And then I got thinking, which can be dangerous. Somewhere, there *is* a church with two bins. And they would get upset if one was removed too suddenly. That's a real life situation.

Let's be prepared to change. It will mean that we will have to grieve for what was and move into unfamiliar territory. We must realise what really matters and reaffirm that the church doesn't belong to us.

Be ready to change. It's vital. And that's no joke.

In Praise of Plass

I'm often asked what preachers, writers and thinkers have influenced me the most in my Christian journey. Asked recently about the Christian book that had most shaped my thinking – the tome of tomes for my 32 year journey as a Christian – I really, really wanted to heap praise on one of the many 'weightier' books that have so powerfully impacted my life. And make no mistake, I have been profoundly shaped by books. Someone once said that 'books are the compasses and telescopes and sextants and charts which others have prepared to help us navigate the dangerous seas of life.' Over the years, the printed page has prodded, comforted, confronted, relieved, motivated and equipped me. And so I wanted to impress with the news that my Christian journey was forever changed by my fireside reading of Calvin's *Institutes*, or by the winsome

⚘⚘

Over the years, the printed page has prodded, comforted, confronted, relieved, motivated and equipped me.

⚘

words of Tom Wright, by thoughtful Alister McGrath or a quick speed-read of St. Augustine's *Confessions*. I wanted people to believe that, as a younger man, I used to sneak behind the bike sheds for a crafty scan of Thomas à Kempis's *The Imitation of Christ*.

The 'heavier' the book, the more impressed some would have been with *me*. I would have actually appeared to be intelligent and might have considered buying some half moon spectacles for my next publicity photograph. Or I could have picked something from the accessible genius of John Stott, or praised some of the more popular books about the church that have shaped my thinking, like *Cinderella with Amnesia*, by Michael Griffiths, or the recently published *Free of Charge*, a beautiful book about giving and forgiving by Miroslav Volf.

But, alas, none of the above is possible and my book selection is going to confirm the caricature that some might have of me: that I am a funny but perhaps superficial soul, who likes to laugh more than think. So be it. You see, the book that has most impacted my Christian journey was not written by someone who lives in a university, chats with their wife in New Testament Greek, or is dead. It is: *The Sacred Diary of Adrian Plass aged 37¾* and is written by, you guessed it, Adrian Plass.

When the book was published, it had wings, flying off the shelves for a very good reason. Plass touched a nerve. He opened a window and let some air in to the musty room that was (and sometimes is) the

> Plass touched a nerve. He opened a window and let some air in to the musty room that was (and sometimes is) the Christian church.

Christian church. He drew back the curtains, let in some sunlight and in that warmth, he revealed some of the pomposity and madness that goes on in the name of Jesus Christ. Thousands breathed a sigh of relief as a result and I was one of them. The book went on to sell over a million copies and was printed in a number of languages.

The Sacred Diary came out in 1988, which was quite a year for the world. A gerbil was elected President of the Student Union at the University of East Anglia, Reagan was in the White House and a Toronto man was found not guilty of killing his mother-in-law when the jury accepted the defence theory that he drove fourteen miles to her house, hit her with an iron bar and stabbed her while sleep-walking.

In 1988, I was a bright young (or younger) Christian thing, keener than mustard, brimming with enthusiasm but not overloaded with too much common sense. Already in Christian leadership, I was armed and highly dangerous with my huge King James Bible and decorated with a Christian badge the size of a dustbin lid. Ready and indeed eager for martyrdom at a moment's notice – or so I thought – I was passionate about evangelism, which I assumed meant assaulting total strangers with biblical information while (a) not pausing for breath and (b) not waiting for a response from them – unless their response was, 'What must I do to be saved?'

I looked certain even when I wasn't, feigned joy when I was depressed and was beginning to feel that I was accumulating more questions that answers, with nobody to ask. I was nervous: neurotic even. Obsessed with knowing the will of God, I was terrified of making any decisions, lest I tumble off the tightrope upon which I teetered. I knew that God loved me but wasn't so sure he liked me. I lived with the secret fear that despite all his affirmations of affection, he was really just waiting to catch me out so that he could gleefully consign me to an eternal barbecue. I had 'given my heart to Jesus' but despite that great transaction, it was still heavy. My brow was furrowed and my intensity bordered on the fanatical. The good news was not sounding or feeling that good to me.

And then along came this flawed yet smiling soul called Adrian Plass, with his doubts and embarrassing temptations, his big follies and little triumphs and his mixed motives and pretensions. What grabbed me by the heart was his wonderful brand of self-deprecating humour. I devoured the book, laughed out loud and cried with relief. Suddenly, as someone still very much under construction and therefore imperfect, I felt included. Most of the Christian books that I had read up until then were filled with gallant faith heroes, knights with shining leather Bibles who countered all opposition with a smart-missile style prayer. They were all swashbuckling pioneers, probably able to recite the whole of Leviticus from memory. Whatever they were, they were certainly not made of the same stuff as me. Or Plass.

> ❧❧
>
> **What grabbed me by the heart was his wonderful brand of self-deprecating humour.**
>
> ❧

Plass caught me off guard. Humour usually baptises us with truth while we are unaware, because we're too busy laughing. But we can learn as we giggle and the usual barriers are down. And Plass's gift of empathy revealed a rare humanity and fragility. Mostly he laughed at himself and in so doing his words stripped away many layers of religiosity from me in a way that forthright preaching could probably never do.

At first I laughed at him and then I found myself laughing at myself. But the greatest revelation was that God really, really liked me, despite my capacity to sin – as well as be stupid, as Adrian frequently is in the book. I discovered that some of my desire for greater faith (a worthy ambition) was little more than hopeful charis-magic. When Adrian tried to move a paper clip an inch by faith, a kind of starter course in relocating mountains, I saw myself. Not only was his description hilarious but it was a mirror. I was so desperate to experience God's power on Monday mornings as well as Sunday mornings. The paper clip had never moved for me either.

I also saw myself painfully exposed in Plass's ambition to be regarded as a spiritual giant by the other members of his church. Here was the mingling of genuinely godly ambition tainted with fleshy human pride. He really did want more of God but also wanted others to take note of how much of God he was getting. Suddenly my own driven passion was revealed for what it really was: not all bad but not all good either. In fact, I realised that we are all a mixture. Robert Duvall played Sonny, a loud, passionate but tarnished Christian leader, in the 1997 movie *The Apostle*. Here was an earnest, godly, deeply flawed man. When interviewed about the film, Duvall was asked if the character he played was a charlatan or a sincere believer. Duvall defined what grace is when he responded that Sonny was able to be both at the same time. Plass revealed that good people do bad things and bad people do good things and that all of us are a combination of the two. Through it all, we are deeply loved. That is the greatest surprise of all and one that will take eternity to get over.

I smiled and smarted when Plass introduced the character of Mrs Flushpool. She is the epitome of domestic Phariseeism, an unsmiling busybody, the arch self-appointed critic and scourge of her church and of her long-suffering husband. But she was not always that way. Beneath all of her religious twittering beat a sincere but damaged heart. I realised that I was often like her, my zeal hijacked by unkindness, a Pharisee who never consciously signed up to join that irritating group but was so squarely convinced by my beliefs that sometimes I lost sight of people and the insights that they have.

I discovered that some of the best Christians are the ones who don't easily fit in. In *The Sacred Diary*, Plass's son Gerald was the irreverent type who unerringly popped his dad's pretentious bubbles but also had a real heart and concern for the underdog and genuinely loved God. Gerald was occasionally outrageous, yet often very wise. We typically think that our children's job is to learn from us. Plass kept being educated by his son and in real life, I have been blessed with a similar education.

> ≼≽
>
> I discovered that some of the best Christians are the ones who don't easily fit in.
>
> ≼

And with all his questions, Plass taught me how to ask them – not with the intensity of a rant, as if the problem is about everyone but me but with the gentle smile of the one who knows his own frailties. G.K. Chesterton famously wrote to the London *Times* about what's wrong with the world. His letter read

Dear Sir, I am.

Yours sincerely, GKC.

Plass pokes fun at the world and the church (on his website today he describes himself as 'a bemused Anglican') as one who has no illusions – he is as much a part of the problem as everyone else. He bravely tiptoed into an area that few Christians are willing to talk about: a married man becoming attracted to a fellow believer and wanting to take responsibility for her discipleship as a result. He really likes the lovely Gloria and gently lets us know that we are not impervious to these temptations. Especially in close knit communities of faith, where words of love and intimate sharing are common, we can find ourselves having our heads turned in the wrong direction. Through it all, Adrian's wife Anne (in the book) is a steady rock of sense and sensitivity, long-suffering and loving.

The book did more than relieve me – it released me. I decided to live the rest of my life enjoying laughter, relishing questions, celebrating small victories and insisting that heaven was smiling in my direction. I finally accepted that my weird sense of humour was not something to be shunned or ashamed of but that I could help others sometimes to laugh for laughter's sake and hopefully to grow as well. If anyone doubts the need for more smiles, then look around at our grey world, so burdened by angst and bad news. Call me a joker if you will. I don't care. Plass's book helped me to be who I am; it was an unlocking and I abandoned a cell to which I will not return. I was refreshed, prodded, provoked and hugged through Adrian's pioneering bravery.

But this book changed me for two other reasons. When I met Adrian and Bridget Plass, I discovered far more than people who have a clever imagination and a flair for words. They are both winsome and kind; in the times that I have shared with them over the years (always too few as far I am concerned) I have always left their company feeling that God likes me more than ever.

And then I owe Adrian a debt for his personal encouragement; he first nudged me into writing. After listening to a set of teaching tapes I recorded about the Father Heart of God (in which I bellowed and yelled about the tenderness of the Lord), he telephoned me and said, 'Write this stuff down.' The result was my first book and he was kind enough to write the foreword for it.

The American writer Christopher Morley once said, 'When you sell someone a book, you don't sell them twelve ounces of paper and ink and glue – you sell them a whole new life.' *The Sacred Diary* was much more than a great laugh. Through those pages, Adrian's willingness to share his pain, his stumbling along, sometimes faithfully, sometimes faithlessly and his commitment to love Jesus even when Jesus seems nowhere to be found, touches my life still to this day.

Adrian, I'm grateful.

Don't sweat it

Yesterday I was sent on a mission. Kay dispatched me to the supermarket in pursuit of a packet of guacamole mix, which is something you add to avocado to produce bright green slime. This stuff looks good with salad but it's reminiscent of that yucky ectoplasm in *Ghostbusters*. The aisles of the supermarket were crammed with eager, mutant ninja shoppers, some of whom were steering their trolleys with attitude. They niftily manoeuvred those unwieldy wire contraptions with the deftness of a Grand Prix racing driver. I wanted to join in with the fun but felt that a great big shopping cart to carry a single packet of guacamole mix was slight overkill.

The checkout queues were long, so I headed to the express line, reserved exclusively for those shoppers with no more than ten items. Two or three people were ahead of me, including an elderly chap whose basket seemed suspiciously loaded. Had he not

&ßß&

The aisles of the supermarket were crammed with eager, mutant ninja shoppers.

&ß

seen the gigantic sign hanging over the till that implied that anyone with more than ten items would be hung, drawn and quartered? My eyes narrowed. As he placed each of his purchases on the shiny black belt, I counted them under my breath.

Seven, eight, *he's still legal but only just.* Nine, ten, okay Mister, you've reached your limit now . . . eleven, twelve, alright, this is really pushing things, *thirteen, fourteen, FIFTEEN!* Someone arrest this man! He is over the maximum limit by a whopping 50%!

How come the checkout lady was smiling so benevolently at this blatant criminal? Did she not know we had a fifteen item monster in our midst? My feet were tapping, my brow was furrowed and a roar of outrage was building inside me because of the awful injustice of it all. And suddenly I stopped and saw myself, a grown man hot and bothered by being kept waiting a whole twenty seconds, or however long it takes to scan five items.

And I wondered how often churches are destroyed, friendships are irreparably harmed and marriages disintegrate because we are so good at being bothered about things that don't matter. Like the Israelites of old, who allowed a man to divorce his wife for burning a meal, too many of us spend our lives armed to the teeth with a magnifying glass, making minutiae massive. Molehills grow to Everest-sized proportions because of our obsession with having things done the right way, which usually means *our* way. Woe betide the unfortunate offender who says the wrong thing, looks at

> ◌◌
>
> **We cover our tracks by kidding ourselves that we are pefectionists.**
>
> ◌

us the wrong way, or does anything to mess with our Sinatra-like determination to have life *My Way*. We cover our tracks by kidding ourselves that we are perfection-ists. Perhaps better words to describe our behaviour would be *selfish, immature or arrogant*.

And we Christians can take pickiness to an Olympic level. Not many churches get into conflict over major issues of doctrine. But if the drummer plays too loud on Sunday morning, the version of the Bible used is not *my* version or, God forbid, someone actually rearranges the chairs, or (tantamount to the blasphemy of the Holy Spirit) the vicar suggests relocating or even removing the pews then the Third World War will likely break out. Being people of conviction that we are, we are quick to adopt the unyielding stance of Martin Luther who, as champion of the Reformation, famously cried 'Here I stand, I can do no other.' This is a statement of greatness when you're defending the doctrine of justification by faith but not terribly appropriate for an in-congrega-tional punch-up about what colour to paint the church toilets.

Sometimes I wish that there was a Bible verse that said 'Lighten up, my people' or 'Chill out, says the Lord.' Perhaps the closest thing available is Jesus' rebuke to the Pharisees because they gave their attention to what didn't matter while ignoring what was vital – picking gnats out of their drinks but gulping down camels (Matt. 23:24). The book, *Don't Sweat the Small Stuff* has sold millions and rightly so: we need to save our perspiration for what counts.

But as I finish writing this while seated in yet another aeroplane, I am appalled to report that the man seated next to me has just sneezed without covering his mouth, probably contaminating my drink with his germs. Not only that but he's just leaned over and read what I've written about him. Yikes. I'm calling the flight attendant. This man must be ejected from the plane, minus a parachute, right now . . .

Embarrassed in Alaska

My nervousness kicked in when the minibus pulled up. We were in Skagway, Alaska and we'd decided to splash out and take a tour of the glaciers in a small single engine plane. Now we were waiting to be picked up for the short ride to the airstrip. The courtesy minibus skidded to a halt. It had seen better days, had probably been previously driven by Moses and was in fact a bucket of rust. I hoped that the company maintained their planes more effectively than their minibuses. But when the driver informed us of our next stop, my heart sank. 'We're going to pick your pilot up on the way out to the airstrip', he said. 'He's at the bar with his girlfriend.'

'We're going to pick your pilot up on the way out to the airstrip', he said. 'He's at the bar with his girlfriend.'

Yikes. Now I was going to hand my life over to a company that owned a bus that was in need of a Christian burial, to be piloted by a man who might well be high and not just in terms of altitude. We pulled up outside the bar and a blond, blue-eyed twelve-year-old (so it appeared) hopped in and introduced himself as our pilot. My palms began to sweat. We were his only passengers. I stifled an overwhelming temptation to hurl myself out of the moving bus and began sniffing the air to try to detect the slightest smell of alcohol. I must have looked like one of those drug detection dogs with hay fever.

Five minutes later, we screeched to a halt at a plane that could have made a guest appearance on *The Antiques Roadshow* and reluctantly climbed aboard. The pilot's door didn't fit, so he had to slam it three times. I wondered how easily it might reopen, mid-air.

'You guys okay?', he shouted back at us. I wanted to scream that no, I was not okay, that I needed to get out of this death trap and that I had mistaken this excursion for a jet-boat ride. But I did none of these things. I gave the thumbs up and smiled a terrified grin. As we taxied down the runway, a pilot in a plane following us radioed our adolescent captain. 'Your brake light is out, buddy.' Great. What else was out? Had he filled up with fuel? Was the propeller screwed on tight? How was it that our pilot was handling an aircraft when he hadn't yet used a shaver?

But we took the flight. And we did so for one reason alone. I didn't want to embarrass myself by protesting. I couldn't cope with the thought of offending our pilot – as young as he was, he'd probably be scarred for life by experiencing such conflict prior to puberty.

As it turns out, there was nothing to worry about. There were a couple of hairy moments, like when he turned round to adjust our headsets while steering directly at a mountain. Then, when he spotted a couple of mountain goats, he flew in very close to see them. But the flight was one of the most exhilarating experiences of our lives, with breath-taking views of the lakes and ice formations. And our pilot was very accomplished and will probably do well as an adult.

I was also stunned as I realised the power of embarrassment. I preferred to risk my life rather than protest. And I won-

∾∾

I preferred to risk my life rather than protest.

∾

dered how much embarrassment paralyses and silences us everyday, when we should speak up. It happens in church life. We go along with the consensus and keep silent when we feel uncomfortable, because we fear that we will appear stupid, unspiritual or rebellious. Red-faced, we shuffle along with the crowd. In some churches, meek compliance is a prized characteristic, especially demanded of the women. Those with a brain cell and a voice are unjustly tagged as 'strong women' or 'pushy.' Some stay quiet rather than risk the embarrassment of the labelling.

So perhaps it's time to take a risk and not one that involves flying. Stop cringing and speak up: kindly but without fear. Feel free to say no if no is what's needed. But whatever you do, don't be embarrassed to death.

One of those days

I was always terrible at French in school. I was scared of my teacher, Mr Peckett (I jest not) who used to deal with any misbehaving pupils by whacking them with a slipper. My classroom naughtiness meant that I went through a phase where I probably had a rubber imprint of a shoe sole on my backside. I used to amuse myself by lobbing orange sherbets around the classroom, hence the regular thrashings. Now I can throw an orange sherbet with precision but my French language skills are limited, which means that I can ask the time and also say *yes, no, hello, thank you* and *Eiffel Tower*. Oh and *baguette*.

> ৵৵
> I was always terrible at French in school.
> ৵

But there is also one French phrase that has stuck in my head through the years and that is, 'Which way to the railway station?' How I have longed for the day when I could utilise this most precious part of my education. Whenever I have been in France, I have hoped to be able to pop this question but, alas, the opportunity has never arisen, because either (a) I already knew where the station was or (b) I was driving. Then there was the added problem that, even if I actually needed to locate the station, I wouldn't understand the reply anyway. I've never been able to use my precious phrase.

That is, until today, in London. A couple of French students approached me and asked, in very broken English, the way to a street in Victoria. With delight, I suddenly realised that this was my moment, when I could actually utilise the sentence *the way to the railway station*. Thirty-four years after learning it, this was my time. Delighted, I opened my mouth to reply and promptly forgot the phrase. I mumbled something in a garbled combination of French and English, the exact translation of which was probably *Turn left at the what is the time please and then right at the Eiffel Tower thank you no hello*. They smiled and were polite but I could see that they thought me to be in need of professional help. They moved on and I missed the moment I had prepared for over three decades earlier. Rats.

Of course, that episode was of no consequence, unless you happened to be a French student lost in London. But it got me thinking about other, seriously big moments: loaded minutes that have changed a lifetime. A decision made in a second can be like a rudder that turns a huge ship, setting our destiny for decades, launching us into great blessing or untold misery. What if young shepherd boy David had not been sent out with the bread van, which led to his epic punch-up with Goliath and eventually took him to the throne? On the tragic side, what if he hadn't spied Bathsheba taking a bath? How would history have been if Moses hadn't been plucked out of the bulrushes and then raised in the royal court of Pharaoh? What if Peter and his pals had decided that a

55

safe career in cod was preferred over an uncertain future with God?

> ❧❧
>
> **Tomorrow could be a day loaded with significance.**
> ❧

Perhaps in an average lifetime we might experience only a dozen or so of those epic days. The problem is that we don't know which ones they are. Great opportunities or searing hot temptations don't usually book an appointment or call ahead. Tomorrow could be a day loaded with significance. What we can do is pray that God will give us wisdom when those days do show up.

Of course, God is steering us, whether we're conscious of it or not: C.S. Lewis says that, for the Christian, a secret Master of the Ceremonies is at work. That should comfort rather than paralyse us: we don't need a simple trip to pick up some fish fingers to launch us into a time of prayer and fasting concerning whether we go to Tesco or Sainsbury's. Not only is that neurotic but it would mean that we wouldn't have time to go shopping and we wouldn't need the fish fingers anyway . . .

But today and every day, we ask for wisdom to know what is right and courage to do it. Who knows? It could be one of those days.

20/20 vision

Visiting the optician is more fun than going to the dentist but only just. With the optician, I don't have to look into the wildly staring eyes of a masked man whose mission in life is to shove forty pounds of stainless steel equipment into my mouth. But there are still bits of the annual eye test I don't enjoy.

For one thing, these days they shoot you in the eyes. Twice. Admittedly, it's only a puff of air fired at high speed but I still have to place my chin on what looks like an instrument of high-tech torture for the shooting. 'No one likes this part' smiles the optician, as if this is supposed to make me feel better. It's painless enough but it always makes me jump. Asking for a piece of wood to chew on during the test seems pathetic. But I do like the part that follows the shooting: choosing new glasses. If I had the cash, I could be to specs what Imelda Marcos was to shoes.

⋙⋙

It was with mixed feelings that I went to the opticians yesterday.

⋙

So it was with mixed feelings that I went to the opticians yesterday. There was no sign on the door that warned me that my day and in a way, my life, was about to change. Junction moments don't come with advance notice, as we have seen.

Within moments, I was chatting to Gary, the store manager. He sported a broad, genuine smile and made conversation that went beyond slick sales patter. Inwardly I made a note to myself: this man is likeable. Talking with him was a pleasure.

Our nattering about optic fields of vision and designer frames gradually dried up. I asked him how he got into the eyesight business. He paused for a moment, seemingly weighing up whether or not to get into his story.

Married with two adult sons, Gary had been a high school teacher and a sports coach. His eldest son (also his best friend) was a keen cyclist. An oncoming driver had fallen asleep at the wheel and ploughed into his son, killing him instantly. Gary had abandoned his teaching career and relocated to Colorado with his wife to be with his younger son. He'd taken a job in an optician's clinic. This was impressive parenting. But there was much more to come.

Gary went on to tell me how he'd gone to the trial of that slumbering driver – a young man of about the same age as his dead son. He'd pleaded for leniency with the judge. Everyone makes mistakes, Gary said. No drugs or alcohol were involved. Ruining that young driver's life wouldn't bring his son back. The judge, stunned, had been lenient.

But then Gary told me how he and his wife had befriended the driver. Not only had they forgiven him but the two families had become close. And now he talked with obvious pride about the man who killed his beloved boy: 'He's going into the air force and training to be a pilot', he beamed, genuinely delighted.

I struggled, unsuccessfully, to keep tears back. I wanted to know his secret. How does someone forgive so magnificently? 'It's my faith', he smiled. Gary is a Christian. Without any threat or clumsiness, he asked me if I was a follower of Jesus too.

Grace shone through: not just in the details of Gary's story but also in his telling of it. There was no overplay, no sensationalism, just a matter of fact miracle. And he didn't attempt to gloss over the pain: 'I still cry every day' he smiled, blinking rapidly, perhaps preventing more weeping.

Heroes make hard choices: they cry but refuse to allow their tears to blind them. They refuse to stop

≫≫

I struggled, unsuccessfully, to keep tears back.

≫

loving, they don't give up on giving and won't let their lives be preoccupied with their own pain. And in giving grace, they find an endless supply of it. The oil doesn't run dry.

Thanks Gary. I met you because I needed a shot in the eyes and some new lenses. But since bumping into you, I see things – and life – much more clearly.

Ouch

Praying for people who are unwell has never been a feature of my ministry. I believe that God still heals today and I am bewildered by the idea that we don't need physical healing any more because we've got the Bible. 'Cheer up, Doris, you may have had your leg amputated but at least you've still got Leviticus . . .'

Over the years, I've hurled up a few thousand requests for those struggling with their health but with dubious results. There have been a few positives but I went through a stage when it seemed that the sick got sicker as a result of my praying for them. I considered approaching BUPA to sponsor my ministry. And I have been put off by those Bible-toting evangelists who imply that your chances of health are significantly increased if you've got some spending power on your *Visa* card.

> ❧❧
>
> I went through a stage when it seemed that the sick got sicker as a result of my praying for them.
>
> ❧

I've not been helped by those heavy-handed people who sometimes make fervent prayer more like a beating up behind the bike sheds. And although I know that there is a biblical command to anoint the sick with oil, restraint would be helpful. I asked for prayer from one feverish prayer team and they lobbed a whole container of olive oil (harvested in the Holy Land but liquid fat none the less) all over my suit. Not only did I still feel unwell but I looked as if I'd been mugged in a chip shop. These eager types also seem to think that God is more likely to act when shouted at the volume of a jumbo jet taking off, or when language is used that is never employed in any other context. Those healing meetings where people command sicknesses to 'Be gone' make me feel like I'm stumbled onto the set of Hamlet.

Perhaps the pressure on the person being prayed for that worries me most. After healing prayer, the unfortunate victim – I mean seeker – is asked if they feel better. There is a huge pressure to affirm that you do, particularly if you're standing on a platform being watched by four thousand people, all of whom are desperate for a result. A pushy leader shoved a microphone under the nose of an allergy-sufferer and insisted that he was 'whole' now. I was secretly glad when, moments after the crowd clapped and cheered, the believer mumbled that he felt wonderful and then sneezed a huge sneeze and pebble-dashed the leader . . .

Despite all of the above, I feel challenged to pray more for and with those who are fighting the lonely battle of illness. A tiny nagging problem recently sent me on a six month skirmish into the uncertain twilight zone of tests and medical examinations. The brief trip reminded me that ill health is a badland to dwell in. My admiration has increased for those who have trudged the rough pathway of pain for years. To take that hike is bad enough – to take

> When someone declares that God has fixed their pain, I find myself immediately wondering if their experience is real.

it without the prayerful support of friends who care is unthinkable. Healing is perhaps an unfathomable but welcome surprise. When someone declares that God has fixed their pain, I find myself immediately wondering if their experience is real – and then, if it is, I then rush to ask why others in darker places are not helped. But despite there being no formula, no sure fire methods and no easy answers as to why more are not healed, we must not be guilty of not receiving simply because we didn't ask.

And when happy breakthroughs are ours, let's celebrate them thoughtfully. A man went forward for prayer at a healing service, his bad back making walking painful. Anointed with oil by the minister, he was declared healed and then told to run across the platform, which he did, apparently without pain. The congregation roared their approval and encouraged, the man legged it to the back of the church and sprinted up the centre aisle. Unfortunately someone had left their handbag in the aisle and he tripped over it and went flying . . .

. . . and broke his ankle. Ouch.

Hope

Tonight I went to what was absolutely the most wonderful Christian gathering of my entire life. That's a big statement to make, because I've sat through a few. I've attended desperately small groups where the guitarist only knew three chords and never succeeded in matching them with any known tune. I've been to large gatherings where virtuoso musicians, dazzling actors and graceful dancers have moved me with their art. I've heard stunning preaching, average preaching and some sermons that have tempted me towards Buddhism. I've agonised through numbing three hour long services where angels probably gnashed their teeth as we sang the same ditty for the forty-fifth time. I've inwardly winced as the worship leader gleefully announced that 'heaven is going to be just like this – only so much longer.' Others greeted his announcement with claps and cheers: I fantasised about assassinating him, enabling him to enjoy the delights of heaven immediately. When it comes to Christian gatherings, I've been to more than my fair share.

But tonight's, without doubt, was simply the best. There were only fifteen or so people there, yet the

◦⑤◦⑤

There were only fifteen or so people there, yet the worship was breathtaking.

◦⑤

worship was breathtaking, the preaching nothing short of epic and the prayers electrifying. Jesus was there, smiling. And so, as it happened, was Santa Claus, splendid in a rich red coat lined with snow white fur. It was an emotional evening; laughter and tears mingled. I even spotted Santa quietly sobbing.

Tonight was Hope's baptism. Hope is eleven and she is suffering from leukemia. The prognosis is very bleak. Save a miracle, there are just a few days left.

Hope and her family know pain. Two years ago, Hope's dad died from colon cancer, at an impossibly young 38. Now Hope's Mum, Diane, is married to lovely Justin, all smiles and care and support. Hope is already a veteran fighter; she survived an earlier battle with bone cancer only to discover that she had leukemia. And so tonight we gathered: parents, grandparents, siblings and friends, to enable Hope to declare her faith through baptism. She is bright and bubbly and looks completely healthy. Her smile is like daybreak, a dawning sun that sends shadows packing.

The sermon lasted three minutes; perhaps more should. Diane, her lovely daughter smiling up at her, told us that Hope believes in miracles but she's not afraid of death. Hope nodded, peace and joy entwined in her. Diane told us that life is but a mist, the Bible says, and that soon we'll all be together. There was no schooled bravado, no rehearsed rigid religiosity: just faith that bubbled over, like clear cold water on a Sahara day. As Diane baptised her daughter, it was a priceless act of worship that stirred the heavens.

Then came the prayers. First, Hope's brothers and sisters prayed out loud, their clear voices thanking God for the gift of her; please let her stay longer. And then Hope prayed; no child spiritual prodigy, just a little girl with faith. 'Thank you for my family and friends. You are an awesome God. I just want your will for me. I love you, Jesus. Amen.'

I had been determined to hold it together. I failed, shoulders shaking. It was a stunning occasion.

⊰⊱

The sermon lasted three minutes; perhaps more should.

⊰

Finally came the goodbyes and the gargantuan grace that is usually only found among those who have suffered much. The family thanked us for coming, kindness spilling over from broken hearts, perhaps unaware of the sign and the wonder that they had just shared with us.

It was then that Santa cried. Isabel, Hope's little sister, was all dressed up for Christmas, in her gorgeous red Santa dress, fur-lined. Her smile is broad too, with the chaotic teeth that make a seven-year-old so delightful. Now, as she hugged her mother tight, tears brimmed over her eyes.

And as we stepped out into the crisp Colorado chill, I remembered that Christianity really is about our forever. Our message is that, whatever hellish bullets life throws at us, there is a God, one who is tough at times to understand but utterly reliable. Death, hell, pain, tears: in the end, he's beaten the lot and we should remember that daily. Someone has said we can be too heavenly-minded to be of any earthly use. They were wrong. There's never been a human being in history who was too heavenly-minded.

Thank you, Hope. At just eleven, you've fully lived up to your name, beautiful little lady. Tonight, with you, we shared faith, worship, joy and grace. Perhaps heaven is going to be like this.

Only so much longer.

A few weeks after this piece was written, lovely Hope Mackenzie Herman died, on January 11th 2008. She lived bravely and beautifully and died fully trusting the Jesus she loved and loves still.

My name is

I recently changed my first name. I did it without much thought, but it wasn't a spur of the moment decision. My name change came after a considerable number of years. From now on, you can call me by my new first name. *Passenger*. Passenger Lucas.

I'm not the first Christian leader to do the name change thing. Yonghi Cho, the pastor of one of the world's largest churches in Seoul, Korea, has changed his name twice. He went from 'Yonghi' to 'Paul' and then switched to 'David'. He seems to be very godly, so one assumes that all these aliases are not to pull a fast one over the Korean tax authorities.

Changing your name can be trendy. There's the talented singer with the mega-mouthful of a name that is 'The artist formerly known as Prince'. But not only does all that seem rather pompous, but impractical. What does his mum call him? Does he

Changing your name can be trendy.

have foot-long business cards? 'The Christian leader for-
mally known as Jeffrey' isn't going to work. Passenger
Lucas it is.

My name change happened spontaneously at
Heathrow yesterday. In my pre-flight fluster, I
approached check in. 'Hello, I'm Passenger Lucas', I
said, without a moment's hesitation. The United Airlines
representative unsuccessfully tried to stifle a smile.
'Good morning, Passenger Lucas', she smirked. 'And
what flight would you be a passenger on today?

I suddenly realized that, because I travel so much, I
have heard so many people refer to me with that tag,
and so I unthinkingly assumed the identity. When I'm
paged in airports, I'm passenger Lucas. When I'm called
to the ticket counter to be told my seat assignment has
been changed, they call me *passenger*. And so I introduced myself by the label that others have given me.

And something similar can happen in life. Our per-
ception of who we are can be systematically shaped by
what others say about us. Labels are designed to stick,
and they can be tough to remove. The child who is pum-
melled by abusive parents, and is tagged as stupid or
worthless, begins to believe that stupid or worthless is
what they really are. The branding hurts. Sticks and
stones may break our bones, but it's not true that words
can never hurt us; sometimes the way that people label
us torments us for a very long time indeed.

So let's be careful of labelling others or ourselves.
Sadly, churches can become labelling machines. In some
tightly controlled congregations, just asking a question
can earn you a label that might never wear off. 'She's
awkward. Difficult.' 'He's shallow. Divisive.' Or we can
label ourselves after a moment of failure. We spin a lie,
but that doesn't define us as liars – surely prolonged
deceit would be needed to earn that badge. And

thoughtfulness about how we refer to people with disabilities is not just inane political correctness, but a vital mark of respect for their personhood. How would I like to be tagged according to my greatest physical challenge? I'm not just among the short sighted with a peninsula for a hairstyle and a crooked nose that can smell round corners: my name is Jeff. Or at least it used to be.

Wonderfully, God does quite a lot of name-calling in Scripture. He has prophetic names for us, like Chosen. Royal Priests. The People of God. The Light of the World, and the Salt of the Earth. Beloved. Elected. Holy. Heirs. Sons. Daughters. God is no heavenly writer of Hallmark greeting cards, and isn't given to vacuous sentimentality. These names matter. Before Jesus stepped onto the battleground that was his ministry, his heavenly Father rolled the clouds back and yelled his name: beloved Son. Dark whispers in the wilderness quickly went for the jugular, and tried to steal his identity. Three times the

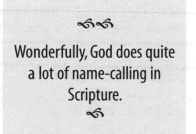

~~
Wonderfully, God does quite a lot of name-calling in Scripture.
~

voice hissed: 'If you are the Son of God . . .' In other words, 'Who the hell do you think you are?' Knowing your name is vital in the war that is faith.

And so despite the frequent name-calling, I'm not passenger Lucas. Who do you think you are? And perhaps there are people that you've slapped a tag on – and it's time to lift the label.

I could be wrong

I tend to be forgetful and can never remember where I left my car keys. But now, thanks to a new gadget, my prodigal keys alert me to their whereabouts. I have one of those key rings that beep when you clap or whistle. I'm impressed by my new key ring and was hoping to mislay it so that I could clap and get my money's worth. My wife thinks I am moving into an ultra charismatic phase: I often march around the house, clapping. Yesterday I put my hands together so much, Kay thought I was working my way through the whole of *Songs of Fellowship*. Then I tried whistling and Kay thought I was having an especially chirpy, happy day, which I wasn't. The keys weren't beeping back their whereabouts to their forgetful owner, because I had forgotten to switch the beeper on.

> ❧❧
>
> I tend to be forgetful and can never remember where I left my car keys.
>
> ❧

The epitome of my amnesia was my forgetting what *country* I was in last week. Americans drive on the right side of the road, while we Brits drive on the left, as God intended. I drove down a busy Colorado street, blissfully unaware that I was not in Sussex and noticed that a car was speeding towards me, on *my* side of the road, or so I thought. I alerted Kay. 'Observe, darling, a deluded chap heading our way. Let us pray that he recovers his sanity', I said. Or something like that.

Still he came right on ahead, like a kamikaze motorist: we were soon to kiss at speed. I was certain he would eventually see the error of his ways and get back onto his own side. About two seconds before crashing, I suddenly remembered: this is America. Perverse as it is, they don't drive on the left. Rats. *I* am in the wrong.

I swerved across the lanes just in time and was appalled to realise that my forgetfulness had nearly caused casualties. At first I thought that I had nearly killed a fellow Christian, since he seemed to be waving at me, pointing a finger heavenward. But then I looked closer . . .

Reflecting on the episode later, I discovered something about me that is a little more troubling than forgetfulness. It had not occurred to me that I could be in the wrong, even though I clearly and obviously was. My reaction was instinctive: I'm right, you're not, kindly move over. Such a deception could have doomed us both to the long term consumption of hospital food, or worse.

And a similar deception can mug us all. We think we're normally right. That uncomfortable reality is the reason for so much conflict in marriages, families, churches and between nations – the notion that we might just have got the wrong end of the stick is unthinkable, particularly for those of us spiritual types who feel that every opinion is downloaded from heaven and that our viewpoint is God's viewpoint too.

Stunning though it might seem, you and I can be wrong and we often are. We are, at times, misguided, misinformed, hasty, unaware, or just plain stubborn. There are only a few short steps from confidence to arrogance. We know the One who calls himself the Truth but then quickly think that we always have the right angle and hold the monopoly on truth too. Some of us occasionally affirm, 'I could be wrong' and then act as if the universe would explode if we were.

So let's face the facts: some of our notions, choices and even doctrines are wrong. And if the thought that our theological viewpoints are not the completely accurate picture bothers us, let's remind ourselves that, this side of eternity, we see but through smeared double glazing, to paraphrase the penultimate verse of 1 Corinthians 13. The Bible is accurate but our understanding of it is flawed.

> ~~
> **Stunning though it might seem, you and I can be wrong and we often are.**
> ~

We'd all do well to think a little more, abandon some of our blustering and sign up for the free but priceless education that comes when we listen carefully to others.

Meanwhile, back in the car, life isn't easy. I just missed my turning and clapped my hands with frustration. The key ring beeped and Kay clapped too and launched into singing *He is Lord*.

And he is. But we're not.

I could *still* be wrong

Men can be irrational creatures, to say the least. One of the more bizarre evidences of weird life on planet male is our deep reluctance to believe what the petrol gauge on our car is desperately trying to tell us. Despite the ominous sight of the white needle hovering just above the 'E', the yellow flashing light in the shape of a petrol can and (in the case of some higher end European luxury cars) the terrifying voice of a German woman booming words like *Achtung* through our car stereo and barking that we are getting low on fuel, somehow we take this as a personal challenge and do everything we can to get home without taking the two or three minutes needed to do the obvious. So it was for me during a family holiday with friends. We were in the West Country and were about to venture onto Dartmoor. Despite the fact that we were moving into foggy, treacherous territory where

❧❧

Men can be irrational creatures, to say the least.

❧

73

the Hound of the Baskervilles roams free, I decided to ignore the fact that we had only a quarter of a tank left.

But that was but my first mistake of the day – there would be a trinity of errors. The second lash-up came when, unsure about our route once we were actually on the moor, I took a turning that I felt convinced was right (because I have an intuitive sense of direction, *not*) and it took us down what felt like a waterlogged pot-holed farm track, which was probably because it was a water-logged pot-holed farm track. We then found ourselves in an area which sported lots of red flags that fluttered bravely along the roadside. We marvelled at the loveliness of the locals getting together for frequent fêtes and carnivals and then realised that we were slap bang in the middle of an army firing range. My confidence that we were on the correct road had led us into a place where we could easily end up in the sights of a goggle-wearing military man in a tank; a chap with a lifelong ambition to fire an armour-piercing shell at a moving target. Like us.

And so now, we were lost on the moors, with the petrol gauge on E, praying that the Lord would miraculously provide us with a large petrol station (preferably one that served cappuccinos) and stranded in the middle of a potential war zone. But there was yet more to come.

We finally made our way back to civilisation (and filled up with petrol) and then noticed a house for sale. We stopped and eagerly jumped out of the car and wandered up to the 'For Sale' sign, which also contained some leaflets that showed the price. Thinking of myself now as an expert in the UK housing market, I turned to my friend and made a solemn declaration of absolute certainty. 'Mark my words, this house will never, ever sell. It's just priced way above the market. These sellers are crazy.'

At that exact moment, a car drew up that had an estate agent's sticker on the driver's door. A suited man hopped out and walked swiftly over to the 'For Sale' sign and tacked a huge 'Sold' board over it as I looked on.

It was then that I realised once again a truth that is unpalatable to most of us and quite unthinkable to some: that is, we can be wrong.

Perhaps we get used to the feeling that we are in the right. The fact that we hold a Bible in our hands, which we rightly insist is the inspired word of God, gives us a sense of consistently being in the know. Then we rush to the conclusion that our choice of music, our understanding of the Bible, our brand of church and our entire worldview on life – in all of these areas we basically are in the right, most, if not all of the time. And while we stubbornly insist on being experts, our churches implode, our marriages erode and others around us take a vow of silence rather than take us on.

> ∽∽
>
> **Perhaps we get used to the feeling that we are in the right.**
>
> ∽

Take notice of the fuel gauge. Read the map. Don't jump to swift conclusions about property prices. In short, know this and it might just prevent you from getting shelled by a British army tank: you could be wrong.

The pace of life 1: Ketchup

Feverish excitement broke out in the Lucas household this week and all because of the arrival of tomato ketchup. A confession like that probably paints us as a sad family that needs to get out more, if we get giddy and don party hats every time the groceries arrive. But this was no ordinary ketchup. The Heinz Company, ever eager to improve on perfection, has produced what looks like an upside down ketchup bottle, with the cap on the bottom. This simple revolution means that the red stuff is always pulled down by gravity and so no shaking is needed and there's no delay when we want to garnish our eggs.

&&

I eat at high speed, as if I'm afraid that someone's about to steal my chicken.

&

The quick-on-the-draw idea was born when Heinz asked customers how their iconic product could be improved. 'They told us the ketchup is perfect the way it is', said a spokesman. 'Their concerns were more about access.' And so the boffins at Ketchup

Central went back to the drawing board and the new packaging means that we now live in the age of spring-loaded sauce. 'Ketchup ready when you are!' chortles the label.

Hallelujah, it's celebration time. As a quickaholic, (my name is Jeff and I haven't got time to tell you my last name), I've always found the two-second shake-and-wait with the sauce so frustrating. I eat at high speed, as if I'm afraid that someone's about to steal my chicken and I prefer the shampoo with the conditioner combined; it saves me time. And speaking of showers, I begin most days slightly damp, because I don't like to hang around to fully dry off. Seconds matter.

When my computer takes longer than usual to download my emails, I twitch. I know that life is a marathon, designed to be a comfortable jog but I tend to tackle it at a sprint. Ironically, by going fast, I end up being late. Trying to squeeze too much in before I drive to an appointment, I calculate precisely how much time is needed for the journey, fret all the way, pray for red lights to turn green and arrive white knuckled, agitated – and late. And I create complicated (and yet more time-consuming)

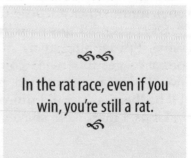

∽∽

In the rat race, even if you win, you're still a rat.

∽

problems by reacting rather than responding, rushing with mad haste to press *send* in response to an irritating email. Perhaps worst of all, life in the fast lane becomes a blur. Laugh out loud moments that should be savoured are left behind in the dust as I move on to the next thing. And prayer becomes text like. Gd. Pls hlp. Now. Amn.

My fear is that I am going to continue to hurtle through the whole of my life at a rate of knots, which will lead to my (premature) death. When they throw me in the grave, my body will thrash around for three days just because of the momentum. My challenge isn't jet lag. I think it's life lag. As Lily Tomlin famously said, in the rat race, even if you win, you're still a rat.

And so I'm asking Jesus, who was not only the Prince of Peace but the Prince of Poise with it, to help me to brake before I break. I can't go on sabbatical, rent a monk's habit and go all contemplative, or abandon my responsibilities. But I can stop to breathe, allow laughter to linger, refuse to allow the schedule to become a god and leave on a journey an hour early so that it becomes a trip and not a race. I can spend more time doing frivolous and useless things, just for the sake of doing them. I can raise a glass to a sunset, go for a walk in the sea fully clothed and read a novel (and not just a Christian one), for no other purpose than relaxation.

Of course, all this slowing down is easier said than done. I'm tapping away at my keyboard furiously in order to get this piece completed before dinner. And now I'm being summoned, prompting faster keystrokes. I'll be there, as per old time ketchup, in two shakes.

Oops, I forgot. No shakes needed.

The pace of life 2: Before you bite

Yesterday I bumped into a rattlesnake and I was nowhere near a zoo. My fanged friend showed up just 25 yards from our front door. Living in Colorado is a wonderful privilege; the sunsets are stunning, the air is clear but the wildlife is just that – wild. Two days before my close encounter with hissing Sid (otherwise known as *Crotalus horridus*) I discovered a tarantula and so am

> ⋖∻⋗
> The sunsets are stunning, the air is clear but the wildlife is just that – wild.
> ⋖∻

now planning to erect a sign: 'Warning: Snakes and Large Hairy Spiders Unwelcome Here. Please go away.' That should do the trick.

At first I was not too perturbed when I discovered the snake, as it was just a baby – about a foot long. But then two unnerving thoughts surfaced. First, where there's a baby, Momma's not too far away and she might well be a little irate if she sensed that her infant pride and joy was under threat. And then I discovered from extensive research (67 seconds on the internet) that the baby rattler is more dangerous than its parents because, when it bites, it has no control over the amount of venom it injects into its prey. And so the victim gets the whole dose. Junior is one dangerous little snake. And old age pensioner rattlers don't settle into a calmer dotage either; some rattlesnakes have been seen striking up to an hour after death. Apparently they just never know when to give up. If in doubt, they bite, even while deceased. It's instinctive.

The most impressive fact is this, if you're impressed by scary stuff: they strike so fast, the human eye can't follow it. You need special laboratory equipment, super high speed cameras, a few dozen willing mice and a head that needs examining if you want to actually see a strike in process, because these critters bite you first and ask questions later. Actually, they never do get around to asking questions.

That got me thinking. Sometimes I get myself into serious trouble, not so much because I'm trying to be bad but because I'm hurtling my way through life at high speed. Life carried on at warp velocity means that everything can become blurred. And then something unexpected happens and, like my juvenile horridus pal, I react rather than respond, with awful results.

The curse of email is an example. How many of us have found ourselves bristling with mild indignation at an unwelcome verbal intruder that lands in our in-box? Breathlessly (and thoughtlessly), we tap out an instant over-the-top response and then press a button, forgetting that tapping buttons can start wars. Send.

Our missile is despatched. And then logic, common sense and basic Christianity suddenly kicks in and we dash around screaming, smiting our breasts and hoping that some way, somehow, we can get our little electronic poison dart back. But it's too late. It's already winging its way through Bill Gates Land and if the victim is online, sharp pain will soon be felt.

We've reacted rather than responded, we've bitten as well as barked and if our strike is about church stuff then we've possibly huffed and puffed so vehemently that we've threatened to blow the house of God down. If we'd just have the grace and maturity to listen, reflect and use a few less words, we'd probably prevent a lot of damage to ourselves as well as others.

Some bites take a long time to heal. Recently a friend told me about a hurtful comment that had been made to him no less than three decades ago. This thoughtless, throwaway criticism was only one sentence long and it took less than two seconds to deliver. Yet he told me that he still occasionally limps today as he remembers those words, especially when he's tired or a little depressed. Some-

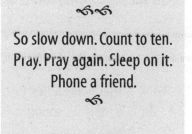

~~

So slow down. Count to ten. Pray. Pray again. Sleep on it. Phone a friend.

~

times the results of our fangs take a lifetime to heal. Sometimes there doesn't seem to be an antidote; the scars fade but never completely disappear.

So slow down. Count to ten. Pray. Pray again. Sleep on it. Phone a friend. And then do something you're less likely to regret.

Meanwhile, back in wild Colorado, I tremble to report that mountain lions have also been spotted in our area. And they've been overheard saying grace.

Mirror, mirror

We were delighted when a pair of starlings picked the eaves of our house to build their nest. We watched in awe as daily their woven masterpiece of twigs and moss took shape, a solid haven against high winds and driving rain. The hatching of two baby chicks turned us into a couple of cooing admirers who are ready for grandchildren, judging by the amount of baby talk that gushed out of our mouths. 'Look at that liddle squidgy fluffy bundle it's soooo cutesy wootsie', I, an adult person, remarked to Kay. 'I know and listen the liddle baby is chirping for its Mummy!', she replied.

It was all lovely until the early morning head-butting began. Each sunrise we are awakened by the sound of daddy-bird, I mean the male starling, hurtling himself at speed against our bedroom window. He peers at the glass, attacks it, momentarily recovers from what is

> ᥦᥤ
>
> 'Look at that liddle squidgy fluffy bundle it's soooo cutesy wootsie'.
>
> ᥤ

probably a nasty headache and a corrugated beak and then repeats the whole performance again. This goes on for about an hour, until the exhausted feathered fighter pilot pops off, presumably for an aspirin and a nap. And he's not the only one who's tired. Our daily dawn wake-up calls are turning us into a couple of red-eyed ex-nest admirers who fantasise about showing 'papa birdy-wordy' the business end of a shotgun (don't write in, I jest).

Extensive ornithological research reveals that our bruised and bewildered friend is not doing this because he had a bad experience with a double glazing salesman. Rather, he sees his own reflection mirrored in our window and, thinking that he's spotted a predator, launches into the flurry of attack. He sees himself – and he senses danger.

And that got me thinking. As I tap-tap at my computer now, I hear once again that dull, repetitive thudding and I wonder what I see when I stare into the mirror – at me. Looking beyond the superficiality of mere looks (for I too am blessed with a corrugated nose), I wonder if I tend to spot the reflection of a good, godly person called Jeff, someone who is basically upright and moral? Perhaps, at times I look at myself with arrogance and pride, especially when I hear of the embarrassing failure or the unspeakable evil of another. Appalled by them and momentarily glad to be me, I become like the Queen in the Snow White fairy-tale, with a 'mirror, mirror, on the wall, who is the fairest of them all?' attitude. I tut-tut at others' sins and silently pronounce that I

> ❦❦
>
> I tut-tut at others' sins and silently pronounce that I could never, ever fail as they have failed and I become haughty.
>
> ❦

could never, ever fail as they have failed and I become haughty and judge them harshly. But, worse than that, perhaps I fool myself.

You and I should realize that the reflection that stares back at us is a mingling of grace and grime. God has touched our lives and made us capable of greatness and love, sensitivity and sacrifice. And yet we can also wound, betray and perhaps be guilty even of staggering crimes.

Isabel Allende describes her realisation of this in her book *Paula*. She says

> Sometimes, when I was alone in some secret place on the hill with some time to think, I again saw the black waters of the mirrors of my childhood where Satan peered out at night and as I leaned towards the glass, I realized, with horror, that the Evil One had my face. I was not unsullied, no one was: a monster crouched in each of us, every one of us had a dark and fiendish side. Given the conditions, could I torture and kill? Let us say, for example, that someone harmed my children . . . what cruelty would I be capable of in that situation? The demons had escaped from the mirrors and were running loose through the world . . .

Knowing that we can each be both beauty and beast should make us a little more willing to realistically assess our fragilities and weaknesses and make us a lot more gracious when others stumble. They are but fellow travellers, companions with us in the holy struggle. Together we daily fight the fallen human condition. We can, in turn, be both predators and saints.

Pecking at my own reflection is a bad, senseless habit. But I do want to learn to look at myself with a mixture of gratitude and soberness. That will save me from some of sin's madness and help me look at others with kinder eyes.

Rob Lacey

Once in a great while you get to meet another human being who is arrestingly different. It is as if they have been given the gift of being able to peer at life through another lens and the rest of us get a wider screen view of our existence from the startling, colourful camera angles that they bring. Rob Lacey, who died in 2006, was one of those people. I remember the day that he came to his first meeting as an advisor to the Spring Harvest Leadership Team and he plunged in with both feet, letting us know that spring was not a time of harvest, a fact that had escaped us all before. We kept the name but realised that having Lacey around was going to be warm, stimulating and fun.

Blessed with the skills of a winsome but incisive wordsmith, Rob grabbed us all by the scruff of the neck with his best-selling *Word on the Street* and did far more than a trendy spring clean of familiar text. As we heard the Creator God of Genesis pronounce 'Fantastic!' about all that he had made, as the forlorn and thirsty Psalmist yelled out that he was 'gagging for God', we learned afresh that God is the Lord who wants to show up in our Monday mornings.

> ~~~
>
> A fabulous actor, with a silken touch for the spontaneous and near perfect comic timing.
>
> ~

Rob's theatrical abilities were well known. A fabulous actor, with a silken touch for the spontaneous and near perfect comic timing, we were entertained and yet nudged and nourished by his one man performances. At one turn, he was like Max Boyce with a Bible, with a deliberately overstated Welsh accent. And then we saw ourselves at our best and worst when he gently sent up some of our worship habits and our passion to sing the same lines over and over, to the point of meaninglessness. But when Rob poked fun, he did so as one of us and his expression was always a smile, never a conceited sneer. He also served as a writer and director, latterly expressing his gifts through the outstanding Lacey Theatre Company.

In 2006, the opening evening in the Big Top at Spring Harvest was given over to a full length play from Rob. The leading character in the piece is Charlie, a pastor whose child is diagnosed with leukaemia. We laughed and cried out loud as Charlie was watched over by a crew of faltering angels, who helped steer him through the darker days. Charlie receives a whole skip load of *Footprints in the Sand* memorabilia, including *Footprints* tea towels, beer mats and even a full sized sandpit with footprints in it, left outside on his patio. We never found out in the play if Charlie's child survived: that was not the point. Rather we were urged to see that when the clouds gather, like Job we can trust God, even if our tiny calculations about life and the universe don't add up. It was as if Rob had gathered us all around his hospital bed, to share with us what he had learned from his trek through cancer, the harshest of journeys.

And he had learned well. His last few prayer letters were written in that same dancing, brilliant style, one of them phrased like a weather report. He was in faith but was not triumphalistic; he seemed

> ȘȘ
>
> **He insisted that we liberate the artists, sculptors, poets, actors and dancers to proclaim, prod, enlighten and inspire us with more than words.**
>
> Ș

at great peace but he very much wanted to live. His daughter, Magdelena, a sister for Lukas, was born just days before his death. Now that he is gone, Sandra and her lovely children must remain solidly in our hearts and prayers.

There is a legacy that Rob leaves us that we must not only cherish but spend well. He insisted that we liberate the artists, sculptors, poets, actors and dancers to proclaim, prod, enlighten and inspire us with more than words. This was not a revolution to overthrow preaching but a call to empower and include those who have often been left stranded in the wings. We must heed Rob's call: action is the best way to honour his memory.

We will miss you greatly, Rob. Heaven must be brighter for your taking to the stage there and the auditorium lights back here on earth have dimmed since you left us. But we will so look forward to appearing with you at the Great Encore to come and the backstage party that will follow. Good night, dear Rob. See you in the morning.

Yell for help

When Kay and I go out to eat in restaurants, there is always a guarantee of live entertainment. This is not because we frequent jazz clubs; it's just that our habit of covertly listening to other diners' conversations has proven to be a winner, real life being more interesting than a show. It's more about people watching than voyeurism but can be compelling. Kay has occasionally hushed me when I've attempted a little natter over the food, on the basis that listening to other people's chit-chat is more interesting than tuning in to me. Perhaps I should buy her some surveillance equipment for her birthday, although I'm not sure that mobile satellite dishes come in pink. During a recent busy preaching tour, I told Kay that I sometimes get sick of the sound of my own voice. She said that she understood completely how I feel.

> ✥✥
>
> Kay has occasionally hushed me when I've attempted a little natter over the food.
>
> ✥

Tonight our dining/spying hobby provided us with a truly fascinating evening. We knew that something a little different was afoot when we pulled into the hotel car park. The place is famed both for its food and conference facilities. We quickly learned that it was packed with delegates who were attending one of those self-help seminars where success in love, life, cash and confidence is guaranteed. We steered around some of the attendees who were scattered around the car park, their brows furrowed in concentration, their hands busy in the act of creation.

They were making things with putty.

We're not sure what their exact assignment was. Were they making the shape that would best represent their emotional state, their favourite animal, or perhaps would symbolise a warm childhood memory or some long-gone trauma? We desperately tried to get a hint from the shape of their putty creations but it looked like all were on a mission to make sausages.

Our dessert was interrupted by one of the delegates, (sporting a 'HI, MY NAME IS JANE!' stick-on badge in thick marker pen) who approached our table, obviously on another assignment designed to boost confidence. 'Hello and how are you both tonight?' she trilled in a terrified voice so high on the octave scale that local dogs were probably howling. She then proceeded to gallop her way through a number of inane statements and questions, her task obviously to engage in a conversation with complete strangers. We were unnerved by her wild staring look and obvious discomfort but we empathised and played along because we knew how she felt. We've been on some evangelism courses . . .

Now I'm not mocking the delegates who had probably forked out large sums in order to learn to help themselves, even if I question the value of sausage making in

> ∽∽
>
> As Christians we return to the core truth that self-help might be helpful but that *we* are not our final resource.
>
> ∽

car parks. I applaud anyone who is on a search for truth, who seeks to understand the mysterious inner space of themselves a little more, or who is doing more than sipping another Heineken and punching the remote for the latest episode of *Corrie*. But while self-awareness, education and development are all vital, as Christians we return to the core truth that self-help might be helpful but that *we* are not our final resource. Jesus drives a proverbial truck through our pretensions and independent ambitions, announcing 'without me you can do nothing', a statement that could only come from a megalomaniac, unless, of course, the Son of God said it. It's good for us to remember that Jesus is not an optional extra, an available resource for the religiously inclined, or a handy help for the sad, limping types who need a crutch to help them through life.

He's the bottom line. The X factor. We were created to know him and without him we are not truly alive or functioning in our fullest potential as human beings. It's not odd to be a follower of Christ. For this we were born, or perhaps, more specifically, for him we were born. Without him, at best, we all hobble.

After coffee and a bit more ear-cupping surveillance, Kay popped off to the loo. Another self-help devotee was in there, a lady who was nursing a bruised and bloodied arm. She'd been taught during the seminar that she'd help herself greatly by karate chopping a concrete block in half. Despite the most fervent concentration, she failed.

Let's not march or meander into independent living. We face the subtle temptation not so much to rebel against God but to just place distance between him and us and live as those who are alone. Let the erstwhile karate lady be a lesson to us all. Living with only self as our source will hurt.

Signs

Thanks to a recent trip to the cinema, I now know what those green-headed folks who live on other planets do with their spare time. It had never previously occurred to me that extra-terrestrials would need hobbies; that there might be stamp collectors and train spotters (or the cosmic equivalents thereof) out there in space. But Mel Gibson's portrayal of an ex-priest in *Signs* has changed all that. Apparently ET and his pals get their kicks by furtively landing their spacecraft in remote rural locations at night-time and then have delirious fun carving elaborate patterns – crop circles – in cornfields. The designs are intricate and look particularly attractive from the air but the sad truth is – folks from other galaxies

✆✆

Their extra-curricular activities amount to little more than agricultural vandalism.

✆

obviously need to get out more. Their extra-curricular activities amount to little more than agricultural vandalism. Weep for our distant friends; they may be able to leap around the universe at warp speed but obviously they haven't yet got *Pop Idol*. If they had, then they'd stop messing about with all those fields and giving poor old Farmer Giles hypertension.

But there's supposed to be a deeper purpose in all of this cereal graffiti. The thesis of the film – and of those who believe that crop circles bear the signatures of non-humans – is that these geometrically beautiful patterns are signs that point us towards a reality of life that is beyond our own. Our friendly local Martians aren't just scribbling at random – they are producing hints that there is something more beyond us.

Come to think of it, the God of the Universe has a similar strategy. Longing to point the way home to a culture of lost souls, he too wants them to be able to read the signs. Sometimes, the sign is a miracle; an explosive, brilliantly fluorescent firework, like a sudden healing or a corpse raised to life. Most of us would love to see more of those firework displays. I hear that God often lights the blue touch paper in far off lands but I long for him to spin a few Catherine Wheels here.

But it seems that much of the time God has more subtle but perhaps potentially more convincing signs. Just today, driving in Northern Colorado, I saw an ingenious marketing device – the human sign. Wanting to short-circuit red tape and evade high billboard charges, a developer pays people to stand on the street corner holding a large arrow that points to the show home that is open for viewing. When the showing is over, the human signs pack up and go home. Very clever.

But not very original, because God thought of the idea first. It was always his plan to use human signs – your life and mine: distinctive, arresting and illuminating because of the quality, integrity, love and laughter that are supposed to be our hallmark as followers of the One who calls himself the Life. I've occasionally heard Christians tell those who don't believe 'Don't look at us, look at Jesus.' Bunk. How else is someone who is meandering around in the fog of lostness supposed to see the invisible Jesus, except by bumping into a life that is resolutely under the command of that same King? And then, as human signs, we are occasionally permitted to speak, to give a verbal explanation for this new wine life that has been handed to us on grace's platter.

> So join me in praying today that our lives will drop a hint, stir a thought and maybe be a direct pointer that leads people to focus on Jesus.

So join me in praying today that our lives will drop a hint, stir a thought and maybe be a direct pointer that leads people to focus on Jesus who is daily scribbling on the canvas of us. We are called to be living signs that make people wonder as they catch a glimpse of the symmetry and geometry that the loving order of God brings. That realisation itself can bring a sense of destiny to our more tedious Monday mornings – we are called to live lives that can be read by the blind.

And if there are any wandering crop circling ETs reading this, then do yourself and us a big favour.

Phone home.

Superstition

I'm never been very superstitious. If a black cat crosses my path, I don't look for so-called luck but just concentrate on steering around it, which I suppose is lucky for the cat. I've never been into crossing my fingers, lobbing salt over my shoulder and touching wood can give you splinters. To me, superstition is faith that got lost. Which is one reason why I find myself increasingly worn out by *Christian* superstition. I've encountered no less than three cases of it in the last week.

A friend told me he'd asked a few probing questions during a house group about some of the more bizarre practices associated with revivalism. As he expressed his rightful concerns buttock-clenching tension filled the room and he suddenly felt tagged as a hardhearted cynic. Someone in the group then prayed that God would 'release him from his theologising' which is one intercession

&ᕦᕤ

Someone in the group then prayed that God would 'release him from his theologising.'

ᕤ

95

that will never be answered, because Scripture insists that we know the truth that sets us free.

And then I learned that God apparently gets upset when certain flags are flown. I've been irritated with a few of them myself over the years, having narrowly avoided blindness during some more enthusiastic services where banners were frantically waved around like windscreen wipers on crack. But God, (I was told), fusses over the emblems that appear on some flags. Attending a conference in a centre that sports the ensign of a particular nation, I heard that someone had discerned that people were tripping over and falling because the Lord was in a flap about the pennant that was flapping. Thirty seconds on Google reveals that the symbol does have a dodgy background. But is this enough to prompt God to allow or set tripwires?

But yesterday's 'revelation' nudged me towards angry despair. A lady who has been unable to conceive and has suffered a number of miscarriages, was told that her struggle was due to her laughing playfully at her father when he danced publicly in worship years ago. The 'biblical' backup used for this hurtful hogwash was the story of Michal and Saul. When David got his kingly kit off and did a sanctified twirl, his wife 'despised him in her heart.' The Bible says that she was barren to the day of her death. Like wild sparks leaping across battery terminals, someone made the connection between an ancient cursing and a modern giggle and, hey presto and hallelujah, they presented a 'reason' for her childlessness.

> ∽∽
>
> Quack solutions and superstitious notions hurt people who are already hurt.
>
> ∽

Quack solutions and superstitious notions hurt people who are already hurt and kick them – in the name of God – when they're down. Mad ideas and behaviour are often proclaimed by 'spiritual' people who claim a hotline to God that the rest of us apparently carnal plebs don't enjoy, thus placing them beyond critique. They can try to put themselves beyond challenge, especially when they teach that anyone who questions them is divisive or even guilty of 'touching God's anointed.'

But worse still is the way that all this portrays God. He becomes a pernickety deity who loathes people who use their minds and their Bibles, who issues a red flag when he sees one that offends him and allows people to trip and who closes the womb of a woman because she laughed when she was a teenager.

I am not saying this because I've become anti-charismatic; on the contrary. My life has been punctuated by wonderful prophetic moments when God truly has spoken to me directly or through others. I raise these concerns, not because I despise the charismatic gifts but because I cherish them. Blindly accepting odd and bizarre statements without carefully weighing them up is not simple faith – it's naïve and even lazy when we refuse to do the hard work of discernment. And it's disobedient. Scripture insists that we engage in that scrutiny.

We *must* think, reflect, do the hard work of examining what the Bible says and always be willing to ask tough questions. The genuine activity of God isn't fragile: it can stand up to the strictest examination. We live out our faith, not in the silenced corridors of the cult where the word 'Why' is frowned upon but in the warm sunshine of the community of God where sane conversation is encouraged.

The baggage police

I had just settled myself on board the plane and was relishing the thrills to come during the ten hour transatlantic flight. We would all be treated to a reassuring safety presentation (what to do when a few thousand tons of metal successfully lands in the sea and floats) and then, once airborne, we would all play 'the mystery food game.' This involves every passenger trying to figure out what on earth they are eating, or at least which food group it hails from. I glanced nervously at the passenger seated next to me. On my connecting flight, I had the misfortune of being parked beside a chap who had won a gold medal in the newly recognised Olympic sport of flatulence. He was a banker but had missed his calling, since he could have provided power for a small city. It seemed rude to suggest that he make himself available to the national grid.

I had the misfortune of being parked beside a chap who had won a gold medal in the newly recognised Olympic sport of flatulence.

An elderly gentleman in the seat in front of me was trying to stow his bag in the overhead compartment and during that process, he moved a previously stowed bag about six inches. Suddenly, a woman seated in the centre aisle leapt to her feet and as soon as she opened her mouth, I knew. She was the Queen of Darkness. 'Don't you *dare* touch my bag!' she screamed. 'How *dare* you!' The whole plane went quiet.

'I'm . . . I'm so very sorry', the now distraught gentleman stammered nervously, his face flushed red with embarrassment by the woman's outburst. He'd not tried to open her bag, take it down, or slip a stick of dynamite into it – he'd just moved it up an inch or two, a perfectly normal procedure.

The Queen of Darkness obviously hadn't snacked on any children that day and was eager for blood. 'Don't you dare touch that bag again' she shrilled. Just then her husband reappeared and within seconds I realized that these two deserved each other and that their two bedroom Transylvanian semi was not a happy home. 'If you touch our bag, you'll have me to deal with' he shouted at the now traumatised man.

I had had enough. I had bitten my lip for too long; I didn't want to get into a fist fight; it doesn't look good when Christian leaders are imprisoned for causing an affray and besides, I'm allergic to pain. The flight attendants were oblivious, preoccupied now with seating other passengers with the aid of an electric cattle prod. It was down to me. I chose my weapon, stood up and waved at the nearest flight attendant.

'Excuse me, can you tell me where to stow my bag?' (That was a fib. Okay, it was a lie. My bag was already stowed). The flight attendant looked confused. What did I think the overhead baggage compartment was for, a sleeping compartment for supermodels?

> My contribution to the moment was probably clumsy and wrong.

I continued, the whole section of the plane listening now. 'I know, that's where I'd normally put it. But I'm a bit nervous today . . . you see, *the baggage police* are on board.' The flight attendant smiled. The old man giggled. And the Queen of Darkness and her consort looked fit to burst. My contribution to the moment was probably clumsy and wrong: but someone had to do something. Their territorial control-freakery was ridiculous.

As is mine some of the time. I am challenged that there might be areas of my life where I clearly send a 'hands off' message to others: you touch that, I break your face. Have I set up machine gun emplacements around parts of who I am? Is there anybody to who I have issued an 'Access all areas' pass? What happens if someone tiptoes onto the 'keep off the grass' area of my cherished opinions? Have I insisted that my way of doing church may not be the only way but it's the best way and God must like it, since I do? And then there's my busy schedule. I discover that sometimes what really matters in my days is what seems to be an interruption at first glance.

Meanwhile, here I am, back on the plane. All through the night, the terrible pair have been glaring at me. There's nothing else for it. I've lost some weight recently and am feeling lithe. I'm popping up to that overhead compartment for a nap. I just need to move a few bags . . .

Christmas in the springtime

Tonight Kay and I attended an excellent Christmas get-together. I'm part of a gang of four chaps who meet quarterly to talk, watch films, pray, eat, drink wine, eat and then eat some more. Every year we get together with our wives for an annual Christmas soiree. And this evening had all the ingredients of a perfect seasonal gathering. There were no chestnuts roasting in an open fire but the crackling logs created a festive atmosphere and a delicious smell. The conversation was warm and humorous and we took the opportunity to review the last year. It was a great Christmas meal.

There was just one prob-lem. The Christmas tree at the hotel was not only dead but long buried, because our Yuletide event took place in March, on Maundy Thursday, to be exact. The Queen was in Ireland dish-ing out dosh, Christians everywhere were hopefully searching out fair trade

ॐॐ

I marvelled at the idea of messing up Satan's (and possibly Santa's) diary dates.

ॐ

Easter eggs but we were doing the ho-ho-ho routine in Cheltenham.

There was a perfectly good reason for our delayed advent bash. I once heard of a church who were very much into spiritual warfare, (but not quite so much into sanity), who decided to celebrate Christmas Day on Boxing Day, in order, as one member explained, 'to outwit the enemy.' I marvelled at the idea of messing up Satan's (and possibly Santa's) diary dates and tried, unsuccessfully, not to laugh out loud. Our three month belated Christmas celebration was simply due to busyness, flight schedules and the availability of the hotel where we stayed. Confusing the powers of the darkness wasn't what we had in mind.

But sharing a Christmas and an Easter greeting during the same evening got me thinking. I wonder whether card carrying non-conformists like me, who are quite unaccustomed to stained glass or anything that is both ancient and modern, actually miss out on the blessings of the Christian calendar. My unfamiliarity with the Christian seasons, coupled with the earliest Easter in living memory, (whoever decides these things was obviously trying to outwit us all) meant that I found myself just last week preaching on Palm Sunday, whilst quite unaware of the fact – and so I made no reference to it.

Throughout history, God has used the rhythm of the changing seasons as a memory nudge to his forgetful people. As the Jews journeyed through life, they paused at the sacred signposts of a variety of covenantal celebrations, like Passover, Tabernacles, Purim, Rosh Hashanah, Yom Kippur and the Sabbath. Their diaries provided prophetic wake up calls as they remembered that they were more than a bunch of lucky refugees who had escaped from Egypt but were people of purpose with God himself at their helm. They partied and they paused to remember and give thanks.

Their festivals enabled them to re-enact their history creatively. Not only would they hear the story rehearsed in words but they'd participate as players in huge dramas where they were both the actors and the audience. The Passover feast was to be eaten by a people dressed and ready for a journey, with cloaks tucked into belts, sandals strapped on their feet and staffs in hand. And a mass camp-out lasting seven days was called for when the Feast of the Tabernacles was celebrated. It was not enough to hear the story of the nomadic journeying of their ancestors through the wilderness; for seven days the people had to live in booths made of tree boughs and the branches of palm trees. They felt and experienced something of what their predecessors

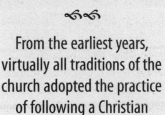

From the earliest years, virtually all traditions of the church adopted the practice of following a Christian calendar.

knew. And something similar happens to us in baptism and Eucharist – not only do we hear words about the wondrous Easter plot-line but we play a major part in the epic, as we are washed in water and the bread and wine touches our taste buds as well as our minds.

From the earliest years, virtually all traditions of the church adopted the practice of following a Christian calendar. Perhaps those of us who are unfamiliar with it should join in.

Meanwhile, I've decided that, in the interests of avoiding spiritual attack from the horned one, that I shall henceforth celebrate Palm Sunday on the Day of

Pentecost, will drive my car in reverse at all times and will possibly change my name to Harold. That'll definitely bewilder hell.

Lethal weapon

The gunman stared at me, his eyes wide and an insane grin frozen on his face. Two seconds earlier a bullet from his rifle had whistled across the breakfast table where Kay and I and our two young children were sitting. Now the room was clouded with the acrid cordite smoke that stains the air when a large bore weapon is fired inside a house. The bullet slammed into the ceiling above the table, showering us with plaster. We all immediately burst into tears, overwhelmed with shock and fear, our ears ringing from the deafening

∽∾

The gunman stared at me, his eyes wide and an insane grin frozen on his face.

∾

explosion. We looked around to see if our children were alive and still had all their limbs. They were unhurt but the gunman wasn't finished yet. There was another bullet still to come.

The day had begun so happily. We had been invited to the home of a minister friend, an Englishman who had

105

relocated to Oregon. He loved every aspect of the back-woods rural culture: big hats, mammoth blueberry pan-cakes – and large guns. He had bought himself a .308 rifle, a serious hunting gun that can kill huge animals and make mincemeat of humans. Eager to show off his dubious prize, he chose to demonstrate it while we enjoyed our bacon and eggs. Thinking that the barrel was empty and that the gun was safe, he cocked it and pulled the trigger. The bullet ricocheted off a wood stove and whistled between our heads. The Reverend Assassin had ignored the most important truth about guns.

Always assume that they are loaded.

Guns aren't as fashionable or available in the UK as they are in America – thank God. Yet each one of us is in possession of a highly deadly weapon. It's called the tongue. Scripture warns us about its fire-power. Variously described as being like a poisonous dart, a viper's bite, a forest fire, a sharpened razor and a sword – and that's not an exhaustive list – the tongue is an efficient little killing machine.

ৡৢ

Stirring speeches end wars and launch wonderful revolutions.

ৡ

With a so-called slip of the tongue, we can annihilate an innocent character with just one shot. Sarcasm can blast a soul's confidence; a well aimed jibe or 'clever' put-down can take someone out. Marriages are slowly murdered by daily murmurs. And then there's the carnage that gossip creates. Strong churches have been scattered and too many vintage friendships shattered by the machine-gun effect of gossip. Careless whisperers place loaded weapons in the hands of any number of people, invite them to pull the trigger whenever they please and then pass the smoking gun on. Your turn; take a shot.

Of course, the tongue can bless too. Words can bring healing, comfort and inspiration. 'I love you' has the sweetest sound. Stirring speeches end wars and launch wonderful revolutions. Martin Luther King announced that he had a dream and oppressed multitudes were galvanized into action. And yet even those who try to use the tongue to help need to be cautious.

To my horror, I've discovered that I can be quite a quick-on-the-draw gunfighter myself. I spend a lot of my life using words, both written and spoken. I love to craft a sentence and choose a phrase to communicate. But any gift that I might have can be used for evil as well as good. In conflict I can be dangerous. Plucking a crucifying comment out of my armoury, I can use words that sting and maim.

Perhaps, because the tongue is so dangerous, God placed it in a cage. And yet still it forms an escape committee. The medieval scholar Estius said of the tongue, 'Though nature has hedged it in with a double barrier of the lips and teeth, it bursts from its barriers to assail and ruin men.'

So, when we speak, let's think first. And, blunt though it sounds, if we're in doubt, let's shut up. Mark Twain was right. A closed mouth gathers no foot. Watch that tongue. Always assume that it's loaded.

Meanwhile, back in Oregon, our gunman friend was not finished with his spree. Shamed and embarrassed by the fact that he very nearly killed his guests, he rushed into the bedroom, ejected the empty shell – and then, flustered, reloaded and fired the gun again, shooting a large hole in the carpet. His enraged wife threw him out of the house.

He's since been allowed back in. But we don't have breakfast plans with them any time soon.

Not as advertised

The telesales lady was almost breathless with excitement. She warbled her shrill congratulations down the telephone, ecstatic that I had been chosen for a 'unique opportunity.' Apparently, I was one of a select few invited to view a brand new timeshare resort in the West Country. We would be rewarded for our time and travel with the free gift of a colour television. This was an attractive offer, as we were about to give our current telly the last rites but I bristled with suspicion. Was she absolutely certain that we'd get the said television, even if we didn't

We would be rewarded for our time and travel with the free gift of a colour television.

buy the timeshare? Were there any strings attached? She assured me. The promotional gift would most certainly be ours. I booked an appointment.

The timeshare presentation was disastrous. A bored salesman showed us around a 'luxury lodge' which was little more than a shed, ideal for housing one's lawnmower but not to holiday in. I pointed this out to the salesman, who sniffed and informed me that these 'rustically luxurious buildings' were Scandinavian in style. But the craftsmanship was poor, there was no view to be had and any Scandinavian who attempted a winter holiday in one of these glorified barns would end up dead or at least frostbitten. We were not interested. The salesman shrugged with the resignation of one who had shrugged much. I asked him where I should pick up my free television.

'Of course. We'll sort you out, as promised.' My heart warmed: these shed builders were at least good for their word. The salesman handed me a small envelope. I'm no detective but I knew that there was no television set squeezed in there. 'Here are the details of the free gift that will be sent to you shortly. Goodbye.' And with a handshake we were swept out of the door – which didn't have a handle to enable any re-entry. I ripped over the envelope, heavy hearted. It contained a mail-in certificate for our telly, which was valued at two hundred and fifty pounds. It was free, except for a handling, postage and packing charge – of three hundred pounds. We had been royally ripped off. The door to the sales area wouldn't open, it didn't seem quite Christian to kick it and burning the place to the ground seemed even less appropriate. We drove home in the gloom of those who have been scammed. The offer was not as advertised.

Do we sometimes do something similar when we tell others what living the Christian life is like? I fear that we can describe the 'product' that is Christianity in a way that is just a little short on truth. I'm not suggesting any skullduggery here but much of the time we talk about being followers of Christ in shorthand vocabulary that sometimes gives a false impression; some more enthusiastic evangelists might risk prosecution under the Trades Descriptions Act. We affirm that prayer is a delightful privilege and indeed it is – but we fail to mention that it can be hard work sustaining what is often a one way conversation. We announce that God has spoken to us and again, he does. But often we don't qualify our words and so others are left believing that we begin our days by tuning into a booming voice in the bathroom. What we usually mean is that we have a sense, a holy hunch and an internal battle, as we ask: is that persistent idea that keeps floating around my head (a) God speaking, (b) the devil distracting, or (c) the after effects of last night's pepperoni pizza? But our quick summaries suggest that we are enjoying 24 hour broadband clarity with the outer heavenlies.

I've sat in too many worship services where an excited leader has quizzed the congregation 'Don't you feel that God is *so* here tonight?' I nod my amen – it seems churlish not to – but the truth is that most of the time I come to worship with absolutely no warm fuzzy feelings whatsoever. My preoccupation is with staying awake, wondering what's for tea or drifting into speculating about what's going to happen in *EastEnders*. Only this

> ⊷⊷
>
> **The truth is that most of the time I come to worship with absolutely no warm fuzzy feelings whatsoever.**
>
> ⊷

morning I sat through a service struggling with irrational guilt because I didn't *feel* more: but isn't worship more about faithful obedience than an emotional high?

So let's be careful about how we describe this life of faith. Let's just tell it the way it is – the good news is good enough and requires no false gloss. I don't want to live in unreality. Life in a draughty shed – without a telly – is a more attractive proposition.

Westminster Cathedral

It was a sombre London day. A gathering gang of angry clouds shrouded the sky and threatened a soaking. I had an hour to spare, was eager to dodge the crush of the Victoria crowd and so I had a choice to make. Should I spend the time nursing an overpriced cappuccino in Starbucks, or sit for a while in the Catholic Westminster Cathedral? After a brief tussle, spirituality triumphed over caffeine and I settled myself in a pew to attempt some minutes of contemplation.

Within seconds, non-conformist prejudices shrilled through me. My mind was assaulted by involuntary harsh thoughts as I sat and pondered the building. I automatically and irrationally hated the opulence, all that marble and the waxy coldness of the statues, with their white, lifeless eyes. My notrils wrinkled at the smell of incense, the lilting tones of the organ did nothing to woo me and my evangelical sensibilities

> ৩৬৫
>
> My mind was assaulted by involuntary harsh thoughts.
>
> ৬৫

bristled at all that genuflecting before the alter. Even the huge crucifix which dominated the nave triggered a tut-tut in my soul; years ago I'd heard an illogical sermon that insisted that an image of the cross should always be empty, since Jesus has risen. So why did these Catholics insist on pondering a broken Jesus? It took me a good fifteen minutes to shut off all the alarms and relax.

How fickle I am, because now I began to thank God for the architects who sought to glorify him with all this grandeur and loveliness. The unusual, pungent incense smelled better now, a signal to the senses that God, the other, the unfamiliar one, was here.

I watched tourists and worshippers come and go and now I was stunned to find myself sniffing with disdain at those who just passed the huge crucifix without a little nod or curtsey. Moments ago, I was dismissing the practice as religious hocus-pocus. Now, I was bristling at those who didn't do it. Judgmentalism is a fire that burns on all kinds of fuel.

It was then that I spotted him. His electric wheelchair trundled awkwardly across the aisle. It was almost a flat bed on wheels, so shattered and twisted was the body of its occupant. His head lolled to one side and it seemed like a supreme effort for him to just look ahead to steer the chair. A large yellow badge on the back of the chair announced that his other car was a Porsche, which obviously it was not. The motorised chair purred to a halt in the aisle and the man twiddled with the joystick, until at last he swung round, facing the altar. He seemed to stare at the smashed, near dead Jesus on the cross for the longest time, a terribly broken man looking up at a wonderfully broken man. No genuflection was possible for him. And then, with supreme effort, he raised his trembling arm and he saluted. His act of worship completed, his arm fell back down again. I marvelled. Every second of life for the man is a trial. Pain and struggle are his constant companions. Yet still he salutes; he is a sign and a wonder.

But then I realized that I was pondering a portrait of what worship always is. My deformities are not as obvious as those of my unknown friend in the chair but they are still very much there. I pondered my entangled motives, the dark thoughts that sometimes slink around dingier corridors in my mind and, as I had especially discovered in the cathedral, my Olympic ability to judge and condemn. Whatever God has done in me, I remain as one under construction, still in process. I too salute, not as one who is sleek and rippling with strong, chiselled muscles, a spiritual body builder but as a member of the fellowship of the bruised and broken. And I come to the God who knows what it is to be shattered – for me. I don't need to wait to worship until tomorrow's victories, or even the greater maturity that might be mine next year. The old hymn is a warm salute from those who boldly draw near to him, in the midst of their fragilities:

> ♠♠
>
> **But then I realized that I was pondering a portrait of what worship always is.**
>
> ♠

Just as I am, without one plea
but that thy blood was shed for me
and that thou bidst me come to thee
O Lamb of God, I come.

I stepped out of the cathedral and looked up at even darker clouds that seemed to boil with rage now. But I had a hint of this; that beyond those enraged clouds, the sun still shone.

There you are . . .

The rocking motion of the London train had nursed me to sleep, my face scrunched up uncomfortably against the chilled, dark window. Suddenly my twilight dreaming was shattered. The man sitting across the aisle was yelling – at me.

'WHAT'S FOR TEA?' he roared. He was staring right into my eyes, demanding an answer but I couldn't for the life of me remember inviting him for a meal. I opened my mouth to tell him that it's impolite to show up at a stranger's home for food, unless you happen to be Jesus talking to a tax man who's up a tree. I stammered something about not knowing him from a bar of soap but he continued his interrogation, seemingly impervious to my words.

> ❦❦
> 'Have you got any lettuce?' he shouted. 'And what about the pickle?'
> ❦

'HAVE YOU GOT ANY LETTUCE?' he shouted. 'AND WHAT ABOUT THE PICKLE?' I started to speak again, to tell him that I was indeed well stocked when it came to salad items and Branston and then I realised what was going on. He was not giving me a culinary cross examination or gate-crashing my salad; in fact he wasn't talking to me at all. The Bluetooth earpiece attached to his head showed that he was chatting to someone on the telephone, one who was apparently lovingly tossing a salad far away. But the volume of his voice suggested that he didn't have much faith in the connection. He yelled so loud that extra terrestrials on Jupiter were probably checking out the contents of their larders. 'DO YOU WANT ME TO PICK UP A CUCUMBER?' he demanded. I really wanted him to pick up a gag.

For twenty ear-splitting minutes the awful, tedious conversation continued. The whole carriage learned that fresh beetroot is great with chicken, that a granary loaf would be nice and that a sauvignon blanc must be well chilled. Never in my life had I known such a public salad. Some of the passengers huffed and puffed at the high volume intrusion. Others nudged each other and giggled. When the conversation moved onto the moral dilemma of choosing vinaigrette dressing over mayonnaise, I feared that some of my fellow travellers were considering forming a lynch mob and that the extremely loud man had eaten his last tomato.

As the ranting continued, I realized one sad fact: this chap was about to enjoy a good meal but he was utterly oblivious to others around him. So preoccupied was he with his creature comforts, he failed to notice that those around him were really *not* interested. If self-preoccupation was an Olympic sport, he'd be getting a gold gong.

All of which challenged me deeply. Sometimes I march through life, furrow browed and focused and can fail to bestow on others that which is so simple and yet so precious: the gift of noticing them. But when I work hard to remember a name, or pause for a few seconds to smile and genuinely care, it can make someone's day. Sometimes I fear that I'm like the ranting caller opposite me; I am so set on what is unimportant that I fail to see the huge needs that are all around.

A dear friend has taught me a simple discipline that helps me to avoid the crassness of self-obsession. Whenever he walks into a room to meet people, he makes a decision, not to mentally say, 'Here *I* am' but rather 'There *you* are.' This simple little mantra has helped him – and now me – to get out of the temptation that nips at us all: the fixation with *us*. Jesus was a popular party guest and not just because of his nifty ability to provide gallons of vintage-tasting wine. He looked past labels, prejudices, sins and scandals and saw *people*. He noticed. People's worlds were changed.

> ❧❧
>
> I am so set on what is unimportant that I fail to see the huge needs that are all around.
>
> ❧

Meanwhile, I'm very worried now. That verbose man sitting across the aisle is staring at me once more and has just announced in ear-splitting tones that he can't wait to finish the salad, build a fire and snuggle up next to me on the rug. I'm really hoping that he's still phoning home.

Fixated

This morning I began my day by dashing around our garden, stark naked, my arms flailing around like windmills, yelling at the top of my voice. Fear not and don't bother to call the police, because we live in a very remote and isolated place, so my lack of clothing (and self-control) was witnessed by nobody except my bemused and long-suffering wife. The reason for my temporary and chilly runabout is simple – we've been getting early morning crank calls. And it's driving me into sleep deprived madness, hence the screaming and streaking . . .

> ✥✥
> This morning I began my day by dashing around our garden, stark naked.
> ✥

Every morning the same couple call us, usually around 5.30am, just as the sun comes up. They always say the same thing, over and over. Once they've called, there's no way I can get back to sleep. I just stare at the ceiling, exhausted and angry, fantasizing about doing something quite awful to these early morning intruders. But there's no reasoning with them: they won't listen.

They are pigeons.

Their numbing mantra – all that cooing – is filling me with an irrational hatred. They *are* filthy; pigeons are rats with wings. Allegedly consuming food equalling three times their body weight daily, not only do they wake me up but they have the cheek to pebbledash our house with what looks like lumpy meringue. I am stunned that, as child, I used to visit pre-Ken Livingstone Trafalgar Square and part with cash to feed these most vile sleep vandals. What was I thinking?

A friend suggested that we buy a large plastic owl, with big, wild staring eyes that looks like Jack Nicholson out of *The Shining*. Apparently pigeons are afraid of owls – or so we were told. Ours set up a nest right next to the glaring owl and apparently made him their best friend and sentry.

> ⏤⏤
> I think about pigeons while driving, eating and studying.
> ⏤

I contacted a pest control company, whose website promised a sure-fire solution to pigeon problems. I thought that some moon-suited chaps would rush round to our house armed with a space age hyper sonic device that would send these cooing devils packing with their wings over their ears. Perhaps they could provide a ground to air missile that would obliterate them. No such luck.

'Go outside and shoo them away' said the pigeon 'expert' when I called him. I marvelled at this specialist advice and wondered if he would invoice me for the privilege of sipping at the well of his wisdom. Not much help there, although I suppose my naked sprinting and screaming was a sort of response.

So now I have become obsessed. I think about those feathery invaders far more than is healthy. I find myself day-dreaming about enjoying a full night of uninter-rupted sleep. Then I nod off during the day because I've haven't known the luxury of a restful night for so long. I think about pigeons while driving, eating and study-ing. During a recent transatlantic flight, I actually found myself hoping that the jumbo-jet would slap into a few and thus reduce the world pigeon population by a frac-tion. And here I am, writing about them even now. I am fixated.

Something similar often happens in our relation-ships and in our churches. We latch onto a small issue, allow anger to be fuelled and launch into an ongoing personal crusade. Often what we lock onto is some-thing quite small: the songs we sing, the translation of the Bible we use, the times of our services. The aversion that we have towards compromise means that we don't listen to the opinions of others and before we know it, we're locked into a fight, majoring on minors while a world stays lost. Churches disintegrate, friendships collapse and marriages fall apart – and all because of minutiae.

In *Love in the Time of Cholera*, Gabriel Garcia Marquez describes a marriage that disintegrated over the failure of the wife to put a bar of soap out for her husband: 'Even when they were old . . . they were very careful about bringing it up, for the barely healed wounds could begin to bleed again as if they were only inflicted yes-terday.'

The deepest love, the most veteran friendships, the strongest churches: all these can be shattered by our abi-lity to obsess over what really doesn't matter that much.

And tragically, sometimes our reactions to the incidental are worse than the incident itself; like my early morning indecent exposure.

Lighten up.

Dream on

Their broad, beautiful smiles should belong to two young teenagers who are grateful for a secure, loving family life, where laughter and hope have been their daily bread. They giggle easily and seem utterly devoted to each other as brother and sister. But their story is more about tears. I bumped into Segent (17) and Dawit (12) in Ethiopia recently. Their brief journey through life

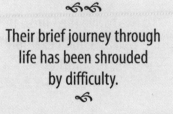

Their brief journey through life has been shrouded by difficulty.

has been shrouded by difficulty, two little people alone in a big, intimidating world.

Segent and Dawit live in a tiny, dark, one room shanty, its bare brown walls enclosing just one bed which they share. Segent has been the primary carer ever since their mother died five years ago from the Aids virus. She took the reins of the home when she was just twelve; the worries and weight of adulthood fell upon her far too soon. Their days are helped by the presence of a Christian run community centre that provides education and basic health care and an occasional lifeline visit from a social worker. Their nights are not so easy. Sometimes they have to bolt the rickety door and hide under the bed, fearful of the rowdy drunks who cavort just outside, wondering if they are coming in uninvited.

I asked Segent what her dreams were. If she could have anything, fairy godmother style, what would be her request? I actually wondered for a moment if the word 'dream' would translate into Amharic. It must be difficult to ponder possibilities when every day is the same numbing, uphill grind. But globalization means that Segent and Dawit are very aware of the world beyond Africa. So would her teenage heart long for an iPod, a boyfriend, or more likely, a one way ticket out of a country where 60% of the population exist on less than 25 pence a day?

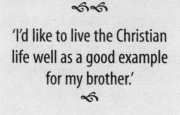

'I'd like to live the Christian life well as a good example for my brother.'

She flashed that dazzling grin again. 'I'd like to live the Christian life well as a good example for my brother.' Both wanted to take career paths that would make life better for their peers. I stared into those bright, shining eyes: this was no rehearsed script to impress the Westerner. There was no hand held out for a cash reward: a few quid for a good answer. They both meant every word. When we left, we prayed together and we gave them gifts. They bowed their heads with embarrassment and I fought back the tears, which would not have helped them. I felt like kneeling before these kids, to humble myself before their lovely hearts.

This was my first visit to Africa and I was taken aback by the extravagant, unexplainable joy that I found there. The poverty is gut-wrenching, the Aids pandemic devastating. The ravages of drought and war have left a country that looks like a post-nuclear attack landscape. But many of the people are just beautiful and it's way beyond skin deep. I'd been prepared a little for their loveliness at a conference in England. We'd played 'Pass the Parcel' and so us Europeans had lingered for a second or two over that wrapped bar of chocolate, hoping to make it our own, all competitive over a 30p item. An African guest finally won the prize and surprised us all with his delighted exclamation: 'Look what we've won.' We tried to explain that *he'd* won it. He didn't get it and unwrapped the silver foil with delight, passing the squares around.

Back in Ethiopia, we wandered into a tiny home where a family of six had adopted the boy next door, who had been orphaned by Aids. Their

❧❧

I cannot deny that I bumped into people who have little to live on and yet really know how to live.

❧

meagre resources were already stretched to the limit, so why add to their burden? Some of these people were not practising Christians, so there was no biblical ethic behind their sacrifice. But they couldn't conceive of a situation where they wouldn't share what they had. Of course, lest I paint Africa as a utopia, we also know that it is a continent that has been beset by corruption, violence and tribal hatred. Sin is certainly international. And yet I cannot deny that I bumped into people who have little to live on and yet really know how to live.

A leading missiologist spoke at a conference recently and suggested that we in the Western church have much to learn from our brothers and sisters overseas. He received an irate letter from a conference delegate, who insisted, 'We have *nothing* (and I repeat, *nothing*) to learn (and I repeat, *nothing to learn*) from those overseas.' It would be laughable if it wasn't so lamentable.

Segent and Dawit face some mountainous struggles ahead. They are at the bottom of the economic pile, disadvantaged and marginalised. But whatever we do, let's not call them poor. With our trivial, Big Brother, techno-obsessed and relationally dysfunctional culture, I think that we are the ones who are really poor.

To find out more, visit www.compassionuk.org